REIGN
OF
GLORY

From
Destructive Dating
to
Magnificent Living

TIFFANY THOMAS

Reign of Glory
From Destructive Dating to Magnificent Living
Tiffany Thomas

Cover Design:
Anointed Fire

Published by:
Anointed Fire

ISBN: 978-1-7331127-8-9

Dedication

To all of the women whom, in every aspect of their lives, our LORD died for His glory to reign.

Also, to generations after them; those who need the souls of the women in their lives to be intact.

To bring forth generations with sound judgment—who are also unbroken and whole.

Reign: To hold official office, sit on the throne, wear the crown, to rule or to prevail.

Glory: Great beauty, splendor, honor, elegance. The manifestation of God's presence.

Acknowledgments

I want to honor my children, Tija and Isaiah,
who suffered as I experienced the events that
led to the revelations outlined in this book.
I'm eternally thankful for the grace of God on
your lives, and for God who, despite my errors,
continues to develop you both into incredible
lovers of Himself and others.

Sincerely, there is no greater joy than to know
my children walk in truth.

Table of Contents

Introduction

Somewhere along the way, we've become perverted. Our mentalities are often reflected on the television show, "The Bachelor", where women have allowed themselves to be placed in positions to compete for men. Our hope is that if we present ourselves as pretty enough, sexy enough, interesting enough, then the man in our sights will find us worthy of winning him.

This distorted practice undermines our innate femininity and is far from what our Creator designed for us to be or called us to do.

By design, the male is the seeker. A lady is to be found. A woman is a treasure. Treasures don't do the hunting. When we find ourselves in pursuit of a man, we are out of order and we're setting ourselves up to be manipulated, devalued, abused, rejected, discarded, and depressed.

What happened to the lady in waiting? Why are we too anxious to wait for a suitor? Why aren't we settled in quiet contentment, finding satisfaction and pleasure with the various aspects of our lives until a gentleman presents himself? I'm talking about a gentleman who meets specific qualifications. One who has submitted his intentions to an authority figure. A gentleman who can clearly state his intentions of courtship that leads to marriage.

How did we become so desperate that we now eagerly and hurriedly give all of ourselves to any man who loosely indicates that he might have the potential to be honorable, and is cordial to us for three months (or usually less)? We give him our all! This includes our bodies, our emotions, our minds, our will, our time, our meals, our money, and our homes. We separate ourselves from our friends, families and everyone of value to prove that we're willing to sacrifice anything to please him. We need him to know that we, unlike those others, really trust him and won't abandon him. We believe and hope with all that is within us that this will prove beneficial for us in time, and that we won't be left rejected and alone. We want him to accept us. Then, we're so confused and angry after he's left without fulfilling any of the things he vaguely suggested that he may do. So, we go back out on the prowl—into the night, across the country, into our contacts list or onto a new dating site to find another man who'll offer the same empty hope as the ones before. This is to medicate the pain of the last ones who have left us empty. Eventually, we end up being emptied and wasted again.

I know because I've been there.

We can do this for a lifetime. I personally know those who are in the winter seasons of their lives practicing this self-sabotaging cycle. We get up, dust ourselves off, buy a new anti-aging cream and a new push-up bra, and we're back on the saddle again! We are so very, very desperate, love-starved, and hungry. We accept almost anything. We hold on frantically to almost anything. We'll literally fight for a mere piece of a man, because to a hungry soul, every bitter thing tastes sweet.

So, we debase ourselves to become the comfort girls, the mistresses, and the wives who are painfully accepting of their husbands' perpetual affairs (not because we're standing in faith believing for the restoration of a healthy marriage, but because we somehow feel that's all we deserve and can obtain). We become the punching bag and the prostitute. We invest far more money than we should allot for this cause. We neglect and endanger our children to get a man.

We believe what we're told, and that is: all the good men are either gay or imprisoned, there's a shortage of men, men outnumber women, and the like. This puts us into a mindset that we must hustle, claw, and scavenge for a man. We do this just to experience some meager semblance of being desired by a man.

We accept the deception that we're incomplete without a man. We accept that we need to have a man with our beautiful, intelligent, cultured, financially self-sufficient selves. Something is wrong with us if we don't have one. We're anxious! We desperately ask, "LORD, when will You send me my man? Where's my man?"
But, hold on. Let's just calm down for a second.

What I want for the women of our time, more than anything, is to abort this practice; after all, it is literally decomposing our spirits, souls, and bodies.

I want us to look at scripture. In Genesis, God caused a deep sleep to fall upon Adam, and He made woman. I believe He did this so that He could cultivate intimacy with Eve; this was so that she could discover who her God is. In addition, this was so that she could understand who He created her to be. So that He could bring forth the beautiful, lovely and unique characteristics that He placed within her. And finally, He wanted her to comprehend that she is a separate entity from her husband.

What if many, many suitable men have remained asleep regarding you because you haven't taken time to become acquainted with the Father and yourself? Until you do, you will continue having the empty gnawing feeling deep within that incites panic at the very thought of not being engaged with some prospect. Until you learn to accept and embrace the all-encompassing, satisfying love of Jesus, the milestones of your life will continue to be marked by horrifically failed relationships. And if you do find a relationship or marriage, he will have become your idol (your god), because you refuse the one true God. You will sacrifice anything and everything to worship your god. You will place demands on him to complete you and satisfy that hollow place within you. You'll be lonely, frustrated and angry because he cannot fill your voids. He cannot. He will be aggravated and frustrated because you cannot be satisfied. Or he'll be obsessed, manipulative, controlling and abusive. None of which is love.

There is salvation in none other than Jesus, my sister. How long will you ignore the truth? How badly does it have to hurt? How unhealthy do you have to become? Your current practices aren't working.

Look, with me, at my experiences and see if you can identify yourself therein. Let's explore probable causes for where we've found ourselves. Let's discover the solution and how to move forward into wholeness and enjoyment of the abundant life Christ died for us to inherit.

CHAPTER 1

Salvation is Come

I cried unto the LORD
by reason of my bondage
Tortured, and in such horrible pain
Crying on my bed, pacing the floor
crying on my bed, pacing the floor

Salvation is come?
LORD, You said
You are the author and finisher of my faith!
What is this?

When both my enemy and I
just knew he had me destroyed
I wept before the LORD, "I cannot take this!"
Devastated and empty
Maybe I'll just drive
Restless and anxious
I'll just drive
Drive through the city

Maybe I'll keep on driving
or lay down on the train tracks
I don't have a gun
but I have access to narcotics
I'm so wounded, LORD, this has got to end

Salvation is come?
LORD, You said You are faithful and true!
…Confused in my mind, scared
can't even process the Scriptures
Unable to discern truth
Tormented!
My idol is gone
Tormented!
My idol is gone. The idol I erected
Intrusive thoughts mounting
LORD, what do I do
What's the answer to this?

"Get up from here,"Holy Ghost said
(And do know that He said, "here"
He didn't say, "there"
God is Emmanuel. He's God with us)
My God is still with me

I got a call from my sister
She prayed with me
She said what Holy Ghost had just said
And, she added sternly
"You better do it quickly!"
Heeding the warning, I sat up on my bed
I wiped my face. I began to exalt the true God

Salvation is come
He is the Prince of Peace
With that peace, I began to declare truth
to repossess control of my mind
"I shall not die
but live to declare the works of the LORD!"
I took authority over my soul
unbinding my soul
Disentangling my soul

…Then I got another call
So, now the mute idol speaks
With railing accusations!
I hung up my phone

Salvation IS come!
He IS the Resurrection and the Life

I started to cast down imaginations
I could literally see
the projectiles of my adversary
I saw myself holding against him
my shield of faith
It was like a big, thick, clear, Plexiglas
rectangular-shaped plate
As I stood behind it, I was safe

Salvation is come! He is strong and mighty!
I gained more strength as I spoke truth
Then, the LORD revealed I had been seduced
by a manipulative spirit
Drawn away; yes, by my own lusts
I was enticed, seduced
so that my enemy could gain control
of my mind, my will, my emotions
for the purpose of silencing me.

Salvation is come. He's my Counselor
I bind my mind to the Word of the Living God
I take authority over my own soul
and command it to bless the LORD
Soul! Why are you disquieted within me?
Hope in God!

Then, the LORD continued to reveal
I had exalted my own self-will
All of my counselors had instructed me to turn
Everybody had told me to run
But no. I decided to disobey and rebel

Thereby placing myself under subjection
to my enemy
The very same enemy
I know wants to destroy me
I supported and encouraged
that which certainly did control
LORD, what is this sickness in my soul?
I've consented to mental and emotional abuse
To be preyed upon, to be wasted and used
I didn't know I was so very confused

Salvation is come. He is my Redeemer
See truth is, that after much, much chiding
yet my refusal to turn
Father gave me over
to believe my own lie
And, I did yearn
For my idol, I did yearn
I thought I had a promise

I had to bring it to pass. I was determined
How I did yearn
I believed the deceiver
because I wanted to believe the lies
And the enemy was pleased
in his foul disguise
And worship. Idol worship
blindness, displaced trust, displaced faith
LORD, forgive me for my displaced sacrifice
God is a jealous God
And He means it when He says that
there is no salvation in any other

Salvation is come. Indeed, He is holy
I began to repent of my
idolatry, rebellion, and iniquity
Now I see the LORD high and lifted up!

Yet, I loathed myself in my own sight
because of my filthiness

I was then also able to understand the stronghold that had been built some thirty years ago
Which had been greatly fortified
by my adversary far more recently

Forty-two months of strong reinforcement
I had to excise that. Cut it away
Declare it dried up from the root
and I eat no more from the fruit of it forever
I had to apply the Blood of Jesus to that
"You are inferior. You are worthless
Void of beauty. You are unlovely. Undesirable.
Insufficient and insignificant"
My enemy accused me constantly
But, do you want to know what?
I am the elect of God. I AM the elect of God
The true and living God

Salvation is come. Full of grace and truth
I had to proclaim that
I am above only and never beneath
The Almighty gave Himself for me
For my ransom
Because He loves me that much
All the work of the LORD is good
I'm His workmanship. I'm wonderful
I'm the apple of the Messiah's eye
He wanted to be with me so badly
that He suffered and died
and went to hell for me

Then resurrected and ascended to Heaven
to go and prepare a place for me
and to intercede for me
Just so we can be together for eternity

Salvation is come. Savior, Rescuer
He knew I didn't have a mind to deliver myself
I thought I'd been discarded
I wasn't discarded
I was delivered by God's mighty hand
and His out-stretched arm
Did not Pharaoh have to let God's chosen go
so that they could worship?
Did not God provoke the whole thing?
So
now, I return with the spoils of war
I stand free. Standing in grace
Rejoicing in the hope of the glory of God
which is revealed in me
Washed with Living Water
with healing in my soul
Finally
Cleansed of my iniquity
I praise my Master for a renewed mind
I am free

I fear not because I know God is for me
He is Jesus
Salvation is come!

…That happened.

Though I rejoiced in victory, and rightfully so, I had only approached the cusp of moving from that dreadful, crushed place. I mourned. I experienced confusion, deep depression, bitterness, unforgiveness, distrust and paranoia. I even returned to that dark place a couple of times. I had to allow the truths of God to renew my mind. I had to discover what caused me to be predisposed to subject myself to that mindset. I had to submit to forgiveness. I had to learn to move forward.

That was a manifestation or, better yet, the symptoms of a disease that had afflicted me long before. Just like a headache can be the symptom of hypertension, or a mass can be the result of cancer; my soul was sick with rejection, shame, abandonment, insecurity, condemnation, low self-esteem, self-rejection, inferiority, deep hurt, and more. Love is the cure. The love of God is always the cure for every ailment of the human soul.

"The heavens are higher than the earth."
Isaiah 55:9

Higher: more influential, powerful, important, very favorable.

The heavens are **higher** than the earth. The spirit realm is preferred over natural things. However, we cannot respect that truth as long as we continue to measure spiritual things using our sensual desires. What I mean is that the part of us that enjoys sin will kick and scream as we begin denying ourselves of what we're used to. We will experience a kind of great discomfort. Yet, as we allow the LORD to teach us to find our satisfactions and pleasures in Him, we'll all wonder why we didn't do that sooner. That which is spiritually righteous is **preferred** over that which is sinful.

There was a time when I found it difficult, if not impossible, to believe. The concept of a satisfying life without a man was beyond my realm of understanding. Some women would tell me about it, but I couldn't imagine being satisfied; I couldn't imagine trading being wrapped up in a man's arms for falling asleep alone. But, I literally stand corrected (and when you discover that too, and find yourself standing, please shoot me an email at morphyou2@gmail.com. I'd love to hear about it).

Our Maker, the One who holds the blueprint, has instructed us to set our affections on things above and not on the Earth. Colossians 3 encourages us, cluing us in to the truth that everything pertaining to our lives is found in Christ. Therefore, to find my life, which is hidden in Christ, I must be willing to identify the characteristics and natural inclinations of my flesh and soul. I must also refuse to be ruled by them. Refuse.

These inclinations are included in the nature of our physical bodies. Everyone has them. You might be prone to fornication, perversion, inordinate affection (meaning a desire beyond which is appropriate and reasonable), idolatry, strong sexual desires, the desire for that which belongs to someone else, and the like. These, and more, reside in the nature of our physical bodies, also known as our "flesh". Yet, when these become the inclinations of our soul, there has been a preceding causative factor.

Let's discuss the soul, and the things that can set us up for corruption to manifest in and from our minds, wills, and emotions. And, if you experienced anything like the debacle I just told you about, please read on.

I pray that the anointing of the Holy Spirit would ride upon these words to give you good understanding, heal your soul, and give life to your spirit. You are precious, significant, desirable and loved beyond what you're capable of comprehending.

CHAPTER 2

Why I Wanted It So Badly

- Rejection

Satan loves to work rejection, insecurity, and the dull, ever-present undertone of self-disdain into women. He does this by using various portals of entry. These entryways may or may not have been particularly huge events. These could include being the product of an unplanned or unwanted pregnancy, an absent or abusive father or father figure, a distracted or emotionally unavailable mother or an authority figure that's seemingly impossible to please. It could be something seemingly benign as unfavorable birth order or the experience of prolonged and irritating nausea while the mother was carrying the baby. Perhaps, one or both parents may have honestly preferred the opposite gender, even though they say they're "still thankful for a healthy baby." Satan can exploit these and countless other scenarios to implant rejection. He'll later send a string of boys (then men) into our lives to further reject us, all the while, flooding our psyche with propaganda. He does this through tales of princesses in great peril who are saved by the handsome prince, romantic comedies where the girl who we can identify with always gets the perfect guy, and depictions of couples who are so very happy all of the time—while we are not. Our adversary does this only to convince us and reinforce the concept that we're insufficient and undesirable. Flawed.

Satan knows that Jesus came that we might have an abundant life. But, he also knows that it won't matter much what's added to our lives if our relationship with ourselves is distorted and tainted. We'll compensate for our dysfunctions and deficiencies by trying to be the prettiest or the sexiest in the room. We'll seek the nicest cars and the biggest houses in the best of neighborhoods. Our jobs will be considered by humanistic standards to be the most significant. Our boyfriends and spouses will outwardly reflect the same. Onlookers will think we're largely successful. Yet, these crutches will invariably fail to provide the healthy sense of self, security and self-approval that we so desperately need. Therefore, even if we attain these superficial things, beneath the surface (after we park the car, greet the attractive man, kick off the heels, take off the bra, wash off the makeup), we'll sink into our four thousand dollar mattress and cry ourselves to sleep, feeling lonely and defeated still.

Just as fear is a spirit (according to 2 Timothy 1:7), wisdom, understanding, counsel and might are spirits (found in Isaiah 11:2), I believe that rejection is a spirit as well. According to scripture, evil spirits have ranking order and varied degrees of power (see Daniel 10:13, Matthew 12:24, and Revelation 9:11). I believe that rejection is what some call a "chief demon" or "strongman" (see Mark 3:27). Rejection is very, very powerful. Satan is so extremely strategic to cultivate rejection in our lives, because ultimately, rejection becomes lodged so deeply within our souls that it cripples us. It hinders us, it keeps us bound up and stifled so that our true selves cannot be expressed. When under the oppression of rejection, the very essence of our beings (who we are at our core), cannot be manifested to carry out the purpose for which we were created. Satan imposes rejection so that we become muted, stilled and impotent. Rejection reduces us to mere disfigured shells of who and what God created us to be. In such states, our environments are unable to appreciate what we were designed to contribute. We're hardly able to connect or flow, with substance, through the lives of those we encounter. Ultimately, the Almighty is prevented from expressing Himself through us. Rejection causes us to produce darkness instead of light. It makes our lives a little more than a sedentary dullness filled with dissatisfaction and discontentment. It makes us afraid. It can motivate us to barricade ourselves behind self-hatred, self-loathing, self-rejection, and deeply rooted shame. This barricading may manifest as a counterfeit outgoing type of personality, or even multiple personalities adapting to perceived audience preferences. Rejection is the overseeing, foreboding and dominating thought; it exercises authority, and it casts a shadow over our very mindsets, words and behaviors. Consequently, we find ourselves incessantly and relentlessly replaying the concept that we are deficient and discarded. It keeps us grounded and lifeless, though we may pretend that we aren't. This is rejection. Rejection is the enemy's plot; it is his most effective weapon of control. Satan launched rejection against us as early as possible to ensure our entire existence would be merely his way of scoffing at our loving Creator. It was launched so that we would pass through the earth's realm incapable of having healthy relationships, although we still live in proximity to, yet still disconnected from the Father, each other, and ourselves.

There is a way out.

The only way out is to fulfill the need. We need the love of THE Father and the power of His

Christ—the Living Word full of grace and truth. Therefore, we need Holy Spirit, who is the Spirit of Truth, to lead us into all truth. The LORD our God is one. His Name is Jesus.

Oh, wretched man that I am! Who shall deliver me? Thanks be to God through Jesus Christ our LORD!
Romans 7:24-25

There is therefore now no sentencing of being doomed for those who are in Christ Jesus; those who follow after the Spirit and not after the flesh. For the law of the Spirit of Life has made you free in Christ Jesus from the law of sin and death.
Interpreted from Romans 8:1-2

As I began to seek Holy Spirit for the extremely deep healing I needed, He began to reveal how the spirit of rejection entered me before I was born. Scripture affirms that this is possible. We see in Luke 1 that Jesus' cousin, John, was filled with the Holy Spirit prior to his birth.

Although I was planned by God and intended from the foundation of the world, my mother was 17 years old when she discovered she was pregnant with me. She was a teen and a high school student who was, of course, living with her parents. My father was the same age and in the same situation.

I'm grateful that my mother didn't choose to abort me, and I'm grateful that my grandparents assisted her with me. Roe versus Wade didn't provoke the Supreme Court to nationally legalize abortion until 1973, the year I was born. Yet, in 1971, abortion was legal in six states. The Centers for Disease Control and Prevention reports there were 615,831 abortions performed in 1973. She could've terminated her pregnancy if she or her parents had chosen to. Therefore, I'm grateful that my mother facilitated my entry into the earth realm.

Nevertheless, I recall asking my grandmother about it when I was a young girl. I'd caught wind from a cousin that there was apparently some scandal involving my conception. My grandmother replied, "We loved you when you got here, but we were very upset with your mother." This statement clarifies the dichotomy of the matter and illuminates how and when the door was opened to the spirit of rejection to enter into me. Although, it's said that I was loved after my birth, initially, I was upsetting. I was a disturbance, if you will. To put it plainly, I was unwanted. Regretted. Rejected.

Satan doesn't play fair. He preys upon the defenseless.

How many people have been left uncovered for rejection to be established within? How many have had negative words spoken over them in their prenatal states, infancy and early childhood? These are those who grow up being governed by the effects of the spirit of rejection as it shapes their personalities, thought processes, and interactions.

Have you ever considered why it seems that people have patterns in their lives? You may notice that a woman who has been raped continues to get raped repeatedly throughout her life, while others are never raped. Or a woman always ends up with boyfriends who obsess over her and threaten her life if she attempts to leave them, while some are never threatened for that reason? I believe the spirit that is the most powerful creates these circumstances to more deeply embed itself and reinforce its access and activity in one's life.

Once rejection attaches itself, it certainly continues to orchestrate situations to fortify its stronghold. I recall as a young child, several of my aunts were simply unkind and unpleasant to me. These aunts made me feel like I was inferior and an outcast. Later, I remember being excluded from social activities in school. I was made fun of by boys I had crushes on. Often, it seemed authority figures and those I looked up to despised me. I was publicly ostracized. Later still, I was rarely chosen to be the girlfriend or one who was worthy of exclusive commitment. I was, by far, more often "the friend". Well into adulthood, I was "the friend". This left me feeling insufficient to receive more, or at least accustomed to accepting the same. I felt rejected. I felt desperate for acceptance, affirmation and camaraderie.

Now, because I've fought many battles with rejection, because I've been engaged with it and wrestled closely with it, I can identify its voice as it continues to attempt to plague me. Rejection speaks, not audibly to the natural ears, but to the inner ear of the heart. Just as Satan spoke to Jesus in Luke 4 when Satan was tempting Him.

Holy Spirit has delivered me, but that doesn't stop rejection from trying to affect me and bring me back into bondage. Rejection suggests that people have ill motives toward me, dislike me, and that people who genuinely love me merely tolerate me. Rejection still attempts to provoke me to withdraw into seclusion, threatening that I'll be rejected by people. But, what I now know is that I'm not rejected, I'm accepted in the Beloved—Jesus Christ.

Please understand that when I say I know I'm accepted, I don't mean I've just read it in the Bible and I can quote it. I mean I've spent time with the LORD, allowing Him to press this reality into my being the way that only He can. The result of this exchange between He and I is a profound, foundational, liberating revelation that has reshaped my being entirely. I know I am accepted. I'm not rejected.

You are not rejected. You are accepted in the Beloved—Jesus Christ.

Having predestinated us unto the adoption of children by Jesus Christ to himself, according to the good pleasure of His will, to the praise of the glory of His grace.
Wherein He has made us accepted in the Beloved.
In whom we have redemption through His blood, the forgiveness of sins, according to the riches of His grace.
Ephesians 1:6

~ Hear the cry of your Redeemer~

One of the symptoms of rejection is the rejected person's need to be satisfied with love, with attention, affirmation, acceptance, and to feel valued, supported and defended. This is a human need that is as important as oxygen and food.

To the little girl who has grown up hiding and trying to mask your insecurities because your father didn't express that you're a treasure, please hear the cry of your Redeemer.

But, if you turn to the arms of the wrong man, (or the governance of ungodly, corrupt church leadership, or the abuse of narcissistic companions or family members) for a sense of identity and significance, realize he will initially use whatever methods necessary to make you comfortable enough to disclose all of your thoughts, desires and fears. Then he will subtly make very clear to you which of your thoughts are acceptable and pleasing to him. This is the training process. He'll begin to manipulate your thoughts to increase his control over you. He'll exploit your fear of rejection, knowing you'll do many things to avoid feeling rejection again.

The unhealthy man will seek to separate you from any source that empowers you to challenge his control, and any voice that competes with his own.

The righteous man will never seek to control you.

Usually, when someone wants to manipulate and control us, they'll initially offer great acceptance and approval. During this phase, we finally feel better about ourselves as a result. Then, they withdraw their approval. Subsequently, we feel confused. We feel badly about ourselves and become even more desperate for their approval. It's a control tactic, meant to keep us emotionally dependent upon them and to further diminish our self-esteem. A person with poor self-esteem is easier to manipulate. A person hungry for acceptance will do almost anything to continue to be accepted once given a taste of what is thought to be acceptance. The wrong man usually seeks this kind of control, worship, and dependency because of his own insecurities and because he is also controlled by rejection.

Regardless of the very real motivating factor behind your desire to feel accepted and loved, please identify the practice of trying to extract love and fulfillment from unhealthy relationships. See it as cancer. See him as your enemy.

Please hear the cry of your Redeemer, and run after God to undo the bondage, the web, and the stronghold of lies. Then, as each fallacy is like a brick, begin to deconstruct the fortress of deception that has kept you mentally and emotionally imprisoned. Discover your real support system. Identify those who infuse you with truth without condemnation. Surround yourself with those who speak life over you with power and authority to increase your strength. Find those who sincerely love you, and will patiently reorient you to truth, build you up and assist you in the renewal of your mind.

Consider that you'll need to evict from your life those who blatantly or subtly make you feel badly about yourself and anyone who diminishes your self-esteem. Avoid people who, after encountering them, make you feel guilty, shameful, unacceptable or insignificant in any way. These are agents of the adversary.

If you realize that you feel confused, this is the result of communicating with a deceptive person. Deception is manipulation. Manipulation is the act of seeking to control. A deceptive person is sent to derail. He will promise many things. He will strategically make statements to incite hope and keep hope kindled. But look at the results that correspond with the promises that he's made. Inspect the fruit of the entire relationship. Is it producing real and actual outcomes? Is it producing frustration, sickness, debt, despair, or disappointment?

If so, my sister, you must cut it off. The only resolution is to separate yourself unto the Father—alone.

CHAPTER 3

The Beautiful Wilderness

Satisfy Me with Your Fullness

I long to be in Your presence
beholding Your face
I long to be in Your presence
knowing Your embrace
I long to be in Your presence
speak to my soul that I may live
I long to be in Your presence
most Holy One

You are the fullness of all my desires
My soul faints for thee
O, wretched man that I am
bound by carnality

The weakness of my flesh
the war against my mind
cares of this world rob me

of our precious time
Chasing nothing has so wearied me
But, Thy countenance makes me free
Until the daybreak and the shadows flee away
I will seek You, Life and Peace

I hear you calling me into Your refuge
In the cleft of the rock, my Lord awaits me
I will open unto You
Only then will I be satisfied
For I shall find my joy, my Joy!

Bring me into thy chamber
Encompass me with Your love
I must dwell in Your secret place
I'm hungry for Your touch

I long to be in Your presence
Where it is You and I alone
I long to be in Your presence
most Holy One.

Ointments of healing
sweet fragrance is with You
My love and my Delight

Draw me to the gratification of your presence
You've sought me through the night

The winter is past, the rain is gone
I've received Your Word
My Salvation, my song
I am Yours
You are Mine, Beloved
The Comforter has come

I must dwell in your presence
I cannot depart from this place
You are my habitation
Teach me to
more intently
seek Your face
I must dwell in Your presence for all time
until time is gone
I long to be in Your presence
Most Holy One

I woke up late for prayer this morning, which
starts at ten o'clock. I was four minutes tardy.
We had a phenomenal time with the Lord who
encouraged each of us. He spoke to provide us

with direction and to answer some of the questions that were on our hearts. He brought a precious transparency among our small group, which inevitably led to a rich conversation after we finished praying. I'm grateful to Him for that. Afterward, I headed to the bank, slightly edgy because I had just a few minutes to get to the bank before it closed at two o'clock that afternoon. Thankfully, I made it! Then, I began the half-hour drive home. I had thirty minutes before I'd reach my kitchen.

Understand this, for three years now, I have attempted to eat primarily plant-based foods. Further, I try to prepare most of my foods at home. Cooking is most cost-effective. Also, when I prepare it, I have more control over what's in it. I try to avoid a lot of chemicals, preservatives and additives. Initially, I asked permission from the Lord to implement a plant-based diet to improve my health because I was really feeling the effects of some of the ailments I'd been diagnosed with. Their processes involve systemic inflammation. So, because I am healed by Jesus' stripes, I'm responsible to discover what I must do to cooperate with Him and bring His healing into manifestation in my body. I believe He granted me the grace and flooded me with the sources of information I needed to enable me to eat this way. Recently, as I considered taking on an omnivorous diet, I believe Holy Spirit instructed me to maintain what I started because He said, "I don't want you to partake of the flesh." Since then, by the grace of God, I've been doing well. However, during my drive home, I thought of all the delicious foods I wanted to eat immediately. Chips, salsa and that yummy queso that I loved were available off the exit to the right. Salsa is made of vegetables. Brisket, I thought. I could get Brisket and Spanish rice with jalapeno cornbread. Ohhh! I could get chopped steak with two vegetables as sides. At least I'll have two vegetables.

What?

Beef and cheese aren't made of plants! Not by the farthest stretch of the imagination, or the most lenient of definitions. What happened to me? You already know—I was hungry. Because I was hungry, I was ready to accept anything to not be hungry. I was willing to consume every forbidden, ill-advised, unhealthy, counterproductive, costly, undesirable thing because I was hungry. In fact, I've been hungry in my romantic relationships too.

…to the hungry soul, any bitter thing tastes sweet.
Proverbs 27:7

Because my soul was hungry, I allowed myself to be the friend, the secret, the side-piece. I was sleeping with people's boyfriends, fiancés, and husbands, begging to prostitute myself and being compensated only by some crumbs of attention. This produced a false sense of acceptance and temporary significance. This was all because my soul was hungry. I just wanted to not be hungry anymore. I needed to be filled.

*For He continues to satisfy the longing soul,
and continues to fill the hungry soul with
goodness.*
Psalm 107:9

Too often, our theology is flawed. My desire is
to challenge the information you've accepted
about God, against what He says of Himself in
Scripture. Do you, like I did, think that God is
some distant extraterrestrial being who is afar
off judging us coldly? A God who likes us when
we do charitable deeds and wants us to go to
church a lot? Is your perception of Him a bitter
one? Do you feel justly defiant against Him
because, after all, He only wants to keep you
from pleasurable things? Have you been miffed
at Him because people who were supposed to
represent Him have mishandled you? Maybe,
you're confused about Him because of things
that other people have said about Him, for
example, the God of the Bible is only for
Caucasian people or the Bible contradicts Itself
and was written and corrupted by man.

If so, I encourage you to read a Christian Bible (one not loosely translated), asking Holy Spirit for understanding and revelation. If you do this sincerely, you will discover the most beautiful story of love ever recorded. That love is for you. God's personable, intimate, deeply satisfying love is for you. His thoughts toward you are good and not evil. He is for you and not against you. He has never rejected you; He gives instruction for your benefit. Anything that you've heard contrary to this is a lie from the evil one. You do have an enemy and he is a deceiver. Jesus gave His life for you. He sent His Word for you to know Him. He sent the Comforter to be with you. What else could He possibly do? God of the Bible makes His appeal to you. Venture to become acquainted with Him. Endeavor to be filled with Him and not hungry anymore.

Therefore, behold, I will allure her, and I will bring her into the wilderness, and speak tenderly to her heart.
Hosea 2:14

We need Him to speak to our hearts to gain a proper perception of Him. Also, He is inexhaustible. The Apostle Paul, who wrote the majority of the New Testament, when telling of what was most precious to him and most pressing in his heart, wrote simply, in Philippians 3:10,

"...that I may know Him..."

Our cry is the same! Oh, that we may know You, Lord!

He longs to reveal another dimension of Himself to us. We ask for grace to continue to position ourselves to know Him in ways we haven't.

Depending on our backgrounds, what's been modeled before us, and our experiences, it's likely that we know the Lord as Master, Teacher, perhaps even Father, Provider and Healer. Yet, there's something very peculiar that the Lord speaks of in Hosea 2:

*And it shall be at that day, says the Lord, that
you shall call me "Husband", and shall no more
call me "Lord".*

To me, this is one of the loveliest Scriptures in
the Bible, revealing the heart of the Lord and
His desire for a tender intimacy with us. All
those relationships listed above hold a different
connotation and paint a very different picture.
"Master" might (erroneously, as it refers to
God) elicit ideas of a cold, distant, dictator with
high demands, lacking empathy. "Teacher"
could demonstrate a wise one in authority
requiring examinations and perhaps
(erroneously still) scrutiny. "LORD", ruler,
apparently even suggests a degree of distance
that He wants to resolve, because this is the
title He used to contrast with the role
"Husband". I fathom that He knows precisely
how He created the convoluted feminine heart
and soul with all its intricacies, and wants
intently to satisfy it.

I believe wholeheartedly that the LORD has not
created a need within His creation that He

could or would not fill. Further, I believe that in this season, He earnestly wants to reveal Himself to you as Husband and satisfy your heart and soul with His fullness. My prayer is that we allow ourselves to be thrust into an experience of romance with the Almighty God. He has chosen you for this and yearns for this warmth and closeness with you. He wants to hold you. He longs to sit and dwell upon the altar of your heart. Only He is worthy.

The Creator of the Heavens and the Earth has an affinity for you. He says that He's given nations for your ransom, and that He surrounds you, cares for you, and protects you as the apple of His eye.

My beloved spoke and said unto me, "Rise up, my love, my fair one, and come away."
Song of Solomon 2:10

I have crowned you with glory and honor.
Psalm 8:5

Doesn't this truth caress your heart in a way that is deeply satisfying and surprisingly real? Why do we feverishly seek mere mortals? Let us abandon our pursuit of mere mortals, because this is exactly what's required. And as we soberly think it over, why wouldn't we? Why do we forsake a present, loving, giving God for man who, regardless of his best intentions, will invariably fail us? Why? Because we're often delusional. Do you think that's too harsh of a word? Do you think it's faulty to describe our mindset and subsequent behavior? When I acknowledge the degree to which I acted like a crazy woman, I must admit that I was delusional. Deceived. Therefore, I'm grateful for the beautiful wilderness and the renewing of my mind. Drawing me into His secret place, He spoke the following to my heart, and He speaks the same to yours:

Now, you will break forth on the right hand and on the left… Fear not, for you shall not be ashamed. Neither be confused, for you shall not be put to shame. For you shall forget the shame of your youth. And though you've given

yourself to many men, you shall not remember the criticism you suffered for being without any of them anymore. For your Maker is your Husband. The Lord of hosts is His Name. And your Redeemer is the holy One. He is called the God of the whole earth. For the Lord has drawn you as a woman forsaken and grieved in spirit. And as a woman who was a young wife when you were rejected, says your God.
Interpreted from Isaiah 54:4-6

Please, I plead with you. Please hearken to the voice of the Lord, your God. He does not disappoint. The more closely you're bonded to Him, the more your life produces life. Only God can bring such deep healing and restore your heart just as if all those experiences never occurred. Allow Him to take you into the wilderness where it's just you and Him. He's the best company! He will teach you that He really is all you really ever wanted and needed.

And you shall always remember all the way which the Lord your God has led you these forty years in the wilderness, so that He might humble you and examine you, to reveal what was in your heart, whether you would keep His commandments or not. He humbled you, and allowed you to be hungry, and fed you with manna- a substance that you did not know, nor did your forefathers know. So that He could make you understand by personal experience, that man does not live by bread alone, but man lives by every Word that proceeds out of the mouth of the Lord." Interpreted from Deuteronomy 8:2-3

Indeed, He's got some words for you. Will you turn your attention toward Him and listen with your heart?

CHAPTER 4

Re-FORM-ation

He Protected the Glorified

…"It's like you don't trust me or something."
the LORD said to me with irritation and
frustration.

Oh, I recognize that I'm supposed to trust Him.
But the matter is,
when we're speaking candidly with
introspection,
I feel like,
"How am I supposed to trust You,
 when you didn't protect me
 against THAT?"

> But, He did protect me.
> He also did protect you.

He provided for me.

He kept me.

Yet, considering promises He made to protect,
there seems to be conflict,
when we consider experiences.

Until we consider this:

1 Timothy 4:8 speaks:
"Physical exercise profits little, but godliness is
profitable unto all things—
having promise of the life that is now,
and of that which is to come."

Physical exercise=
                THE physical exercise=
                The human experience:
                Experiences in the natural realm:

These profit to some extent. Oh, but godliness!
Godliness is where the value is.

THE HUMAN EXPERIENCE IS SUFFERING.

Job 14:1 speaks

44

*Every person born of a woman is of a few days
and FULL of trouble.*

*2 Corinthians 4:16 says
Therefore we do not become discouraged;
utterly spiritless, exhausted, and wearied out
through fear. Though our outer man is
progressively decaying and wasting away, yet
our inner self is being progressively renewed
day after day.*

The only profit gained in this physical
experience—
is to attain more godliness
There is no system in this world that will
produce a sustained
sense of happiness
or satisfaction
But when we learn to be temperate in all things
and take all thoughts captive
bringing them in subjection to Christ
then we can maintain
(laboring to enter into His rest)
our posture in His presence
where there is fullness

of joy and pleasure evermore

We're seeking the correct things
but by the erroneous means
and from improper sources

There is no perfection in this world since
the Fall
Our expectation needs be to discover
His promises
in the spirit realm into which we have been
born
and made alive

Is not Satan the god of this world?

Yet, we can bring, from the spirit realm
things that are to be
and which have originated
in the spirit realm
"In this life, and that which is to come."

But the physical is vastly, ghastly limited
And we are tempted to be deceived:
to live as if this is our home

Surely-
He has protected
and will continue to do so. I've learned
He shall perfect
that which concerns us
until the day of Christ's return

Therefore, He's so patient with me
He knows I'm still in
and contend
with this natural state
and with its natural mind
Hence, He loves me to life
And says,
"Come
Let's reason together."

He wants, and is worthy of my trust
Because despite this human experience
He has given me the earnest
of His Spirit, and will keep me from falling
from being destroyed, and losing the ability
and potential to actualize
who He created me to be:
                Glorified.

And do not be conformed to this world any longer, with its superficial values and customs. But, be transformed and progressively changed as you mature spiritually by the renewing of your mind; focusing on godly values and ethical attitudes. So that you may prove, for yourselves, what the will of God is. That which is good and acceptable and perfect in His plans and purpose for you.
Interpreted from Romans 12:2

Be transformed or reformed by the renewing of the mind.

According to Merriam-Webster, to renew means to make like new, restore to freshness, vigor, or perfection. To make new spiritually: regenerate, to restore to existence, revive.

We must change the way we think. Our behavior is produced by our thoughts. Let's acknowledge that the way we've been thinking and the things we've been doing aren't working, because we can't argue with results.

Now, let's take notice of some identifiers that reveal erroneous thinking. The following are concepts that should serve as warnings of problems or danger. Be honest with yourself, asking Holy Spirit to search your heart. Are any of the following thoughts similar to your mindset?

-For those not in relationships:

*I feel discontent and anxious when I'm not in a romantic relationship. If several, or at least one man is not actively pursuing me, I feel discarded and unwanted, and restless.

*I'm constantly on the lookout for my next potential mate, positioning myself to be noticed and approached.

*Being the interest of a man feeds my sense of self-worth. I feel a sense of pride when a man expresses his desire for me.

*I'm most happy when I'm involved in a romantic relationship. I feel I need a relationship to be satisfied.

*I feel an intense sense of bitterness and sadness when I see couples who look happy, or when I hear of an engagement or wedding.

*I feel like my life is on hold as I wait for a man to want me and to marry me. I imagine going to the places that I'm waiting to go until I'm on a date. I've reserved clothes and other items until I can wear them for or share them with that special man.

*I'm willing to hide my involvement, or to be a secret for the pleasure of receiving attention from a man.

<u>For those in relationships</u>:

*Everyone who loves me and otherwise expresses genuine, unbiased concern for me, counsels me to terminate my involvement with this man.

*Since being in this relationship, my intimacy with the Lord has suffered. I find that most of my prayers are pertaining to the sustaining and advancement of this relationship.

*Since being in this relationship, the closeness I used to share with my family and friends has suffered. I don't mind canceling plans with them for an opportunity to be with this man.

*I find that I'm carrying out increasingly risky and unusual behaviors as this relationship progresses. I'm finding it more difficult to recognize myself, thought-processes, words, and actions. People who know me well comment that I've changed.

*I cannot imagine living without this man. I'd sacrifice anything for him. I find that I'm literally afraid that we might end, and this fear plagues me regularly.

*I regularly experience feelings of fear, jealousy, confusion and anger.

*This man has more influence over my judgment and decision-making than any other source.

*I find myself in defense of this relationship to protect it much of the time.

*If my children and this man were dying, but I had the ability to save either this man or my children, I'd save this man.
Note: This reality might not be a conscious thought, but can be realized by my actions and my willingness to sacrifice my children's well-being (my time, attention, possessions, food, etc. for the man) as well as my lack of properly prioritizing them.

Conclusion:

If you've found yourself in some of these scenarios, know that you are not alone at all. Also know that some of these were very difficult for me to acknowledge as my own mindset, especially after forming them into concrete, tangible thoughts. When they were no longer floating in the abstract realm of my subconscious and as I lived increasingly intoxicated by my fantasies involving men, I was faced with the reality that my own faulty belief-system undermined me. My thoughts supported unstable practices and were thoughts I would've associated with others unlike myself. Although you might feel unnervingly vulnerable, becoming cognizant of your defective thought-patterns, you can celebrate entering into a season of healing and transformation as your mind is renewed.

Be patient with yourself. Don't accept condemnation. Realize that your adversary was tactical and deliberate to inundate you with this broken belief system until you adopted it. Yet, if you ask Holy Spirit to change you, you are changing. If you asked Holy Spirit to grow you, you are growing. Trust the process, although it can sometimes feel unpleasant. You'll appreciate the results of having submitted to the process. Joy and liberty are on the other side.

Meanwhile, allow Holy Spirit to introduce you to the attractive qualities that you possess and be encouraged thereby. Discover some of the characteristics that make you intrinsically yourself. Maybe, you'll find that you're great at interior decorating or that you enjoy writing, painting, poetry, or singing. Perhaps, cycling or running is peaceful to you. Do you find travel exciting? Do you enjoy playing violin or piano? Perhaps, you want to pick that up again. What do you innately enjoy and appreciate? What do you dislike independent of the influence of another human being?

You are complete in Christ.

What are your natural inclinations as you are independent of a relationship? Recapture your own attention and pursue God and yourself tirelessly, with the same dedication and enthusiasm that you pursued a man with. You know it's in you.

It's like reprogramming your default settings. Permit old, flawed responses of the soul to die by performing the system D.I.E: Denounce. Isolate. Educate.

Denounce

Speak against what you don't want. Kill it with your words. Then speak only what agrees with where you want to go instead of where you are. Consider the following scripture about the power of your words and how they set the direction of your life:

A bit in the mouth of a horse controls the whole horse. A small rudder on a huge ship in the hands of a skilled captain sets a course in the face of the strongest winds. A word out of your mouth may seem to be of no account (or, insignificant), but it can accomplish nearly anything, or destroy it.
James 3:3-5 MSG

Do you recall making statements like the following?

- I will always love you.
- I will never be with anybody else.
- I'm yours forever.

Each of those statements and others like them are called oaths. Such declarations don't simply dissipate because your involvement with a person ended. They must be denounced. They need to be verbally disagreed with and spoken against. They must be broken.

The most powerful words we can speak are the words from God or, better yet, the Word of God. In John 6:63, Jesus (who is the Word) said,

"The words that I speak to you, they are spirit and they are life."

Every word we speak is spiritual. Every word we speak is spirit. Each influences our world. Each has the potential to produce either death or life. Jesus has given us Himself so that we may also speak life. You might make a daily declaration similar to the following:

"I take refuge in the Lord rather than trusting in man or in princes, because I understand that

56

man is insufficient to be my safety or my provider or my sustenance. I'm not seeking man's approval. My accuser is cast down. The Lord created my soul. Therefore, only He satisfies it. I submit my soul to the Lord continually. My security is completely in the Lord, and I am secure. I rest in His salvation always. One thing I desire and seek for is to dwell in the house of the Lord all the days of my life to behold the beauty of the Lord and inquire in His temple. The Lord is exceeding abundantly above all I asked for or thought about. The healing virtue of Jesus Christ flows through my spirit, soul, and body. I seek first the Kingdom of God and His righteousness, and I am confident that all other things I'm concerned about will be added to me."

Isolate

This is the practice of literally isolating or detaching yourself from sources that support and reinforce the stronghold that has kept you mentally and emotionally bound. Seek the Lord concerning which relationships you need to restructure or even terminate. Ones that have proven unprofitable link you to your past. They won't allow you to escape the thoughts and practices that you're trying to abandon. These are the thoughts that need to be under strict investigation for dissolution. Additionally, you'll likely need to avoid "chick flicks" and romance novels. Anything that stirs you up emotionally and reinforces that longing for a romantic relationship or dreams of marriage probably needs to be cut off, at least for now. This includes bridal magazines, some Internet sites, fantasy, and daydreaming of being with a man.

Holy Spirit drastically changed my environment as I began to become very intentional and determined to renew my mind. He relocated me to a new city approximately two and a half hours from where I had resided for almost two decades. This was a quick and extreme move, but He provided for it and the transition. It was smooth and exhilarating.

My circle of friends changed, rather became alarmingly minimal as I entered the wilderness. I did have the valuable experience of being very close to the woman who was my pastor at the time. This aspect, I believe, was as paramount and divinely constructed as any of the other miraculous and essential aspects of my relocation, and there were several.

I'm telling you now, that as long as the heir is a child, they're no different from a servant, even though they own everything by order of inheritance. But they are placed under tutors and trustees or guardians until the age declared by the parents.
Interpreted from Galatians 4:1-2

I have been blessed with a few incredible mentors that the LORD has used to deliver me from some of the demons that stifled me, including erroneous mindsets, poor habits, self-destruction, and an awful, gnawing pit of bondage, limitations and stagnation.

Hear me—get under the tutorage of some God-appointed trustees and guardians. This can save your life. Your guardian will help you avoid some pitfalls, missteps, and regression.

Realize that we're not fighting against natural forces, rather closely grappling with spiritual wickedness of great authority. Some of Satan's most powerful weapons against us are isolation, ignorance, deception and fear. We need to be trained. We must be mentored.

That notable prophet and priest who anointed both kings Saul and David was, before all of that, under the governance of Eli.

Now, Samuel did not yet know the Lord, and the Lord's word hadn't yet been revealed to him. A third time the Lord called Samuel, he got up and went to Eli and said, "Here I am. You called me?" Then Eli realized that it was the Lord who was calling the boy. So, Eli gave Samuel instructions concerning what to do next.
1 Samuel 3:1-3

Everyone isn't permitted with us into the Intensive Care Unit. He, alone, is the Great Physician. And even the Great Physician,

Jesus, submitted Himself to His cousin, John the Baptizer.

He heals the broken-hearted and binds up their wounds.
Psalm 147:3

And hearing this, Jesus said to them, "It is not those who are healthy who need a physician, but those who are sick."
Luke 5:31

Aren't you grateful that He cares for sick folk? I am. When I was dying from my diseased soul, infecting everyone in close proximity, He called me into quarantine with Himself alone. It was Holy Spirit calling me away to become acquainted with Him—His ways, His personality, His character, His voice, His peace, His love and His ability to fully satisfy.

I believe there's a time when He calls every believer into isolation with Himself. This is profitable in every way. It can feel strange because many of us are used to having others around in abundance. Often, we use people as crutches. We use people to medicate ourselves for the pain of our insecurities and deficiencies. We use others to distract us from things we need to give attention to. But, He calls us away to experience His healing and relief.

Educate

Out with the old, in with the new. Ask Holy Spirit to inundate you with new, appropriate information. He will do it.

As Holy Spirit began to renew my mind—first, through the Word of God, I was introduced to three main sources that I gleaned invaluable concepts and principles from, all of which can be viewed on YouTube.

I stumbled across (meaning, Holy Spirit orchestrated my finding) Redefined TV. My good friend and I even traveled to one of their conferences in Houston. The presence and power of the Lord there was life-changing to meet the needs of women of all ages, races,

and statuses. Their official site is:
www.redefinedtv.net.

Soon after, I discovered Tiffany Buckner and
Anointed Fire. This woman of God pours out
knowledge, wisdom, and understanding for
hours at a time. I was wide-eyed and amazed!
It was as if Holy Spirit unzipped my cranium
and irrigated my mind and heart while, at the
same time, siphoning out the sludge and grime
of defective belief systems when I listened to
her. She spoke regarding things I thought only
I could've experienced, making sense of things
that had me perplexed. Her official site is:
www.tiffanybuckner.com.

I also began to listen to messages from The
Porch- Watermark Dallas, and their series
titled, "Save the Date" was the first one I heard.
It baffled me and challenged my thinking. It
also confirmed my thoughts of westernized
dating, courtship, engagement and the like.
Check them out. Other great ones are titled,
"Dating Detours" and "The Blueprint for
Marriage". Their official site is:

www.theporch.live.

Most recently I've purchased the book titled, "Table For One" by Irishea Hilliard. This is an excellent read full of jewels. I highly recommend it.

I'd like to point out that being in a local ministry is imperative. Every Believer needs to be involved serving at their church. Because while the resources I've listed above are magnificent supplementation, they cannot replace your physical church and tangible pastor any more than a multivitamin replaces a meal. It is my strong conviction that we should be able to connect with leadership in a real church, not only a virtual one. Our leadership should not only know who we are, but they should know us. Someone should know when we're absent, out of character, struggling, entering temptation, need help getting out of the thorn bushes, need encouragement, need someone stronger to tag team with or just need a hug.

We give very little thought about submitting ourselves to a preceptor at our places of employment, a university instructor, or a senior ranking officer in the military. We even obey the command of our gynecologists. Yet, when it comes to spiritual elders, Satan convinces us that we're to become quite independent, and that it isn't necessary to subject ourselves to those who have matured past the point where we are currently. This is deception. We can find leadership who love God and people, filled with the Holy Spirit, and who've committed their lives to His service, the advancement of His Kingdom, and building the Body of Christ. No person is infallible, yet we aren't searching for idols. By Holy Spirit, we're led to those who are after the Father's heart, and who can nurture us into a greater dimension of Christ-likeness.

Let every soul be subject unto authorities who are more advanced. For there is no power but of God. The powers that be are ordained of God. Whoever resists authority, resists the ordinances of God, and those who resist will

receive to themselves damnation. For authority figures are not threatening to those who perform good works, but to those who do evil. You don't want to be intimidated by their power? Do what is right, and you'll be acknowledged for doing so. The minister of God is for your benefit.
Romans 13:1-4

I've had the honor of working with and being around soldiers of the US Army who've been on multiple deployments to the Middle East. Never have any of them said they'd prefer to go to war alone. Nor would I. Why then would one want to walk alone in a spiritual landmine? There are snipers firing flaming darts from the distance, a brigade of demonic special forces setting up ambushes and a series of airstrikes are incoming. Such a person is about to become a prisoner of war, or missing in action or killed in combat. This should never be.

Incidentally, who among you has also learned that a good hug, when really needed, is a very, very powerful ministry? I recall being in the midst of spiritual warfare trying to be free, believing God for the deliverance that He describes in His Word. I was tired, hurting, beat up on, and confused. By the grace of God, His power and strength, I was still fighting though. I was weary, folks. I sat down in the sanctuary next to a female minister. She instinctively reached to hug me, and I began to weep. I surprised myself by how I wept. I'm talking about ugly face, snot and all. Right there on the pew between services, she just sat there holding me as I cried and released pain, tension and frustration. I walked away healed to some degree. I'd received strength and resolve to continue the battle. I'm sure she prayed for me, but to this day, she's never said a word about it. She didn't take me to the back for counseling with seventeen people in senior leadership; I wasn't interrogated with ninety-two questions. She just held me as I cried. You're not going to get that from a televangelist or Periscope pastor.

The Lord, who instructs all things for our benefit, meant it when scripture reads:

"Let us think of ways to motivate one another to acts of love and good works. And let us not neglect our meeting together, as some people do, but encourage one another, especially now that the day of His return is drawing near."
Hebrews 10:24-25 (NLT)

We need someone close enough to be in the trenches with us. My mentors have proven invaluable and transformative. With them I've tackled rejection and self-rejection, manipulation, jealousy, pride, fear, anxiety, depression and self-righteousness. All the same, the Lord continues to develop me. My mentors have continued to love and guide me even when I am obnoxious. I'm grateful.

I pray that the Lord directs you. I pray you submit to His reset. I encourage you to consent to allowing the Lord to transform you through the renewing of your mind, and that you allow Him to satisfy each area that needs to be filled. He will fill you up as you commit to time with Him.

Your transformation will be revealed in your responses. You'll see it! First, you'll come to love peace. Consequently, you will disallow anyone to interrupt your peace. Having finally known peace, you'll weigh it as most valuable. You'll be able to hear and easily detect threats to your peace. You'll know when a man is fraudulent. Then, you will dismiss that man with utmost decisiveness. It'll be as if you instinctively recognized the deception. This is called discernment. As a result of discernment, you will withdraw your foot from the foolishness.

You'll arrive at the place where you will not compromise your intimacy with the Lord. This type of intimacy takes time. We've bought into the propaganda of fairy tales and men who are eager to convince us that we're in love at first sight, so that they can quickly have their fill of us. After this, they'll proceed to the next woman. But real intimacy—closeness, the state of knowing and being known, understanding, true familiarity—that takes time.

Recently, the LORD made provision for me to purchase a home. As the house was being built, I was impatient. But, wanting that process to be hurried is a foolish thing. Have you ever tracked the building of a house? It's not that it's impossible to assemble the structure in less than four to six months, but rather, there is preparation prior to the laying of the foundation. After the foundation's construction, the foundation must cure before it can be built upon. According to an article in "Hunker" written by Keith Allen, "While full strength does not occur for 28 to 60 days, depending on the conditions, the building process can begin when the foundations are about 50 percent cured." That means for at least fourteen days, it appears nothing is happening. Yet, this period is vital. "Not giving the foundation adequate time to dry can lead to a host of problems. The foundation will settle, crack, sag and not be able to support as much weight as it would if it had been allowed to dry properly." (Source: Common Foundation Mistakes/ myersconcrete.com).

Likewise, it is with each lasting, dependable relationship. Your authentic relationship with the Lord is no different. A real relationship requires sowing and effort. It includes fun, pleasant emotions, shared experiences and work. Gone are the days when I believed I was to meet the prince, be swept off my feet, fall deeply in love and effortlessly live happily ever after. Those are the thoughts and expectations of a girl. I've put away childish things.

My relationship with the Lord is a lovely, exciting, intermingling of my committed devotional time where I may or may not hear any magnificent thing from Him, and following up on a Scripture He prompted me to read, and His expounding on that Scripture, and Him cracking a joke (by the way, you want to see me laugh and guffaw hysterically like a nut, let Holy Spirit tell me a joke), and me wondering why our time together was so dry today, and me telling Him my fears and worries, and Him spontaneously surprising me with some mind-blowing revelation that changes my entire perspective regarding my whole life, and me grumbling about not wanting to get up at 3am when He awakens me, and Him reminding me that He's with me as I watch a movie, or shop for groceries, and me asking where I should get gas or what I should wear that day, and Him telling me not to buy the iPhone right now because He already told me that He doesn't want me to incur more debt, and me lamenting how I should've asked Him what I wanted to eat before I ate that, and Him flooding my understanding with how beautifully perfect He thinks I am and how He delights to express His creativity through me, and how I fill His heart with joy and pleasure, and me trying to maintain of my vehicle on Loop 1604 because I'm sobbing, "Awwww!" with a mind blown by how incredible it is that He thinks this of me, and my asking Him, "Hey! Why have you been so quiet all day?" and Him replying, "Why'd it take you so long to notice?"

All of that. It's a relationship. Our LORD is relational.

All of that takes time. The incredible thing is that relatively, we've just gotten started. We have the rest of my life on this Earth and all of eternity to bond. I love Him so. And He loves you so and wants desperately to share Himself and those kinds of moments with you (or whatever moments that He knows will blow your mind).

I'll interject this here—you may be saying, "But, I do love the Lord. I already seek His face." Yes, and I encourage you to allow Him to explore your heart and reveal any areas that you have kept from Him, and what hindrances there may be. His love is effectual.

No one experiences the presence of the Lord and remains unchanged. Please recognize that being where His presence is isn't the same as experiencing His presence. I'll use myself for example.

From as early as I can remember, even as a young girl, I was constantly distracted from Him. I always knew of the Lord, I always knew

Jesus is the Messiah, I always knew He is supposed to be my authority and I'm supposed to be subject to Him, yet every single time He would begin to become active in my life to settle and solidify me within Himself, I would become more interested in something else.

Get this—for 19 years, I was in a ministry where the Word of God is preached and taught in a very peculiar manner. The richness of revelation and depth of teaching there is sufficient for growth and development. Many of the gifts of the Spirit are in operation. The pastors have yielded their lives for the benefit of those they minister to. Again, I was there for 19 years. Yet, it did not profit me nearly to the extent that it could have because I did not do my part by <u>spending time alone with just the Lord, without the distraction of seeking something or someone else</u>. I refused to enter into the wilderness.

I saw other people come in and grow, and this produced a great frustration and confusion within me. That's roughly 6,935 days. I suffered from self-inflicted spiritual dwarfism. I was spiritually retarded because of my heart's condition. Can you imagine how disturbing it is to see a 19-year-old sitting at the little desk in the classroom full of kindergartners? That was me spiritually. I attended services religiously. Counting Sunday services and Wednesday night Bible Studies, that's approximately 1,976 services I attended. Yet, I was preoccupied with idols. Men who had been strategically sent by the enemy one after another to capture my mind, will, and emotions; this was to prevent me from connecting with the Lord consistently enough to produce fruit in my life or for others.

Remain in Me and I will remain in you. For a branch cannot produce fruit if it is severed from the vine. Likewise, you cannot be fruitful unless you remain in me.
John 15:4

In my life, historically, my adversary used a man to <u>disappoint</u> me.

Disappoint, dis-appoint:

Dis-
Latin prefix meaning "apart" "asunder"
"away"…

Appoint-
Assign a job or role.
Synonyms (include): designate, select, choose,
elect, specify, decree, establish…

Using the preceding definitions, let us
reconstruct the former sentence by saying:

**"In my life, historically, my adversary used
a man to keep me away from my assigned
role and established designation."**

Chances are, if this book ministers to you, our
adversary has used the same tactics to keep
you disconnected from the secret place in
Christ Jesus so that you'll be alienated from
your God-ordained purpose in the earth.

But, no more.

One day, years ago, I told the Lord,

"Father, I'm so disappointed." He responded, "No. You're still appointed." I just needed to eradicate the things that had kept me disengaged from Him and subsequently detached from the role He had designated me for. I was playing another role. I didn't like that role.

Despite your experiences, you are still appointed. As you continue to seek Him and as you are led by Holy Spirit, He will sit upon the throne of your heart. You will begin to know the Lord, and you will begin to adore Him. He will begin to fill you up, and you'll know joy and satisfaction like you've never imagined. And once you do, you'll terminate the conversation of the unrighteous man as he looms to undermine your intimacy with the Lord. You will have never imagined that anything could be so gratifying! At that point, with more resolve than you've ever made any decision, you will choose to preserve the integrity of the closeness that you share with the Lord—even if it means you'll never date again. Either way, you'll be okay with that.

Finally, we abandon our independent quest to get a man to satisfy us, and we'll seek and trust the Lord and His divine plan for our lives. He'll say to you what He's said to me, "You may go after that if you choose. However, you cannot have that and me also. You cannot go in two directions at the same time. You have to make a choice."

Your response will be that the man isn't worth it!

I cheer you on as you taste and see that the Lord is good!

"See what great love the Father has lavished on us…"
1 John 3:1

CHAPTER 5

Give Not That Which is Holy to the Dogs

…Neither throw to the pigs that which has beauty and great price. Because, scripture tells us, that if we do they will step all over it, turn around and tear us down.
interpreted from Matthew 7:6

How many times have we squandered the greatest parts of ourselves and ignorantly tossed our hearts, bodies, ideals, full disclosure, trust, dreams, gifts and talents onto those who simply weren't worthy? God made us holy. He has declared that we are holy, and requires of us that we be holy still.

Holy: dedicated or consecrated to God, and His purpose. Sacred.

If you have been born again you, at your core, are sacred. At the fundamental, basic, elemental aspect of your very being, you are holy. You are purposed to be set aside for exclusivity.

God's purpose for you is excellent.

But, when we lack understanding of who we are in Christ and our purpose, value, and assets, we will indeed give that which is holy to the dogs. According to Easton Bible Dictionary, one of the negative descriptions of dogs are the following:

As the dog was an unclean animal, the term is used as a reproach or humiliation. They would wander the streets, devouring dead bodies.

I've certainly known some men who were predators, lying in wait to consume the dead pieces of my soul. Wandering from one dying woman to another, scavenging. Certainly, we know the ones who pretend to be a "woman's best friend", playing the role of the confidant, supporter and protector. Yet, after some time, he is revealed as nothing more than a dog. Perhaps, this type of man did have honorable motives initially. Perhaps, he genuinely believed he loved me, but the lifeless aspects of his soul disallowed him from maintaining his intentions. I've been guilty of the same because of the lifeless aspects of my own soul. Nevertheless, let us no longer give ourselves to these. You are far too valuable to be foraged. Your purpose is to be treasured indeed.

Therefore, let us submit ourselves to verse seven of that same chapter, which reads:

"Ask, and it will be given to you. Seek, and you shall find. Knock, and the door shall be opened to you."

Ask. I believe we would be doing ourselves a favor if we became more honest with the Lord and with ourselves. Since our relationship has grown into a friendship of intimacy, I have learned to tell the Lord everything: the good, the bad, and the ugly. Before this, however, I found I was embarrassed to admit to Him that I wanted to be in a romantic relationship. As if that somehow revealed a weakness, ungodly desire or it was something to be shunned for or ashamed of. But, God knows our thoughts afar off. With that understanding, the sentiment now goes something like this:

"Lord, I think I would like to finally know the love of a man. Please give me to a husband who is enthralled with you, and will subsequently be enthralled with me because I'm your creation, Your daughter who reflects you. Please give me to a man who You can love me through. But ultimately, what I desire is satisfaction in my soul. So, however You choose to best satisfy me, whatever brings you the most glory, please do that. If it best benefits your Kingdom for me to be married, please let it be so. If it best benefits your Kingdom for me to remain single, please let it be so."

I have no doubt that He will give me that. I have no doubt that I will receive that request, one way or the other. I trust the Lord and His favorable intentions toward me. I know He loves me and only intends good for me.

The second thing that we're learning to do is submit to **seek**; that is, seeking the Lord, not a man, a relationship or marriage.

> *But seek first the Kingdom of God and His righteousness, and all these things will be added to you.*
> *Matthew 6:33*

When we seek the Lord, we can be assured that we will be satisfied with the Lord and what He chooses to add to our lives. This is an attractive promise because He is the only God who is eternal. He is the only One who is lasting, unchanging, self-sustaining and complete. Allowing us to be satisfied with anything less would be unloving and an injustice towards us. It would be a set-up for disappointment, sadness, longing and frustration. Hence, when He tells us to have no other gods before (defined as "in addition to")

Him, He isn't being narcissistic. Rather, this command demonstrates the greatness of His love for us. He doesn't want us on a bunch of roads that lead to nowhere. He died to give us abundant life. That life is found in Him. There is nothing truly desirable outside of Him.

I think of it this way—imagine the Kingdom of God as a tangible kingdom with physical boundaries. Now, imagine the Lord as King. His decree (or Word) establishes the operations of the Kingdom, and His decree is law. He's a good and loving King, providing the needs of those who are under His rule. He is kind, not like a harsh dictator. He takes care to oversee His dominion and rules accordingly. Everything necessary for His citizens to live wonderful, abundant lives is within His domain. But what happens if one of the citizens decides to cross the boundaries of the Kingdom into a land where there is an evil, wicked ruler who wants to destroy that person? This evil ruler likes to throw propaganda to entice the King's citizens to abandon their designated dwelling place. The loving and merciful King sends search and rescue missions to extract and recover the lost citizen. But what if the King's lost citizen is so very dedicated to the idea of finding a mate that the citizen refuses to be rescued, so she remains outside of the Kingdom? The King's protection and provision is drastically limited because of the citizen's decision.

I exhort you, if you have been lured away from the King's love, please discern the rescue attempts and be delivered back to the Kingdom of God's dear Son. In Him, all profitable things exist.

The third thing that we're submitting ourselves to is knocking. When we continue to knock, scripture promises that the door will be opened unto us. **Knock**. Knock upon the stony, hardened places within our hearts and minds that prevent a righteous and fluid movement in our lives. Knock against those things that produce congestion, a damming up, and restriction of the beautiful things the Lord desires to pour into our lives. Knock against the fears, insecurities, unforgiveness, unrighteous ambitions, bitterness, trauma, deceptions and error. Scripture says:

Is not my Word like a fire? Says the Lord, and like a hammer that continues to break the rock into pieces?
Jeremiah 23:29

Within God's Word, there is a solution for every problem. The Word of God is God. When we inundate ourselves with His Word, accurate teachings about His Word and conversations with Him (prayer), He will miraculously give us a new and different way of thinking. The issue is hardly external. The problem is our perspective. It's the way we see, perceive and understand things. The problem is the way we see God, others and ourselves. If we allow Him to change our understanding, our lives will inevitably change. Knock and the door will be opened. The confusion will be sorted. The chaos in our lives will be made peaceful. Our internal unrest will be resolved. We will be satisfied in our souls.

*Every valley shall be exalted, and every
mountain and hill shall be made low. The
crooked shall be made straight, and the rough
places smooth. And the glory of the Lord shall
be revealed (in you), and everybody will see it.
For the mouth of the Lord has spoken it.*
Isaiah 40:4-5

We need only to trust and submit to our loving
Father. And, we know that we can because the
summation of Matthew 7:8-11 says:

*Consider; what man is among you who, if his
son asks for bread, will instead give him a
stone? Or, if he asks for a fish, will instead give
him a snake? If you, being sinful by nature,
know how to give good and advantageous gifts
to your children, how much more will your
heavenly father who, as perfect as He is, give
what is good and advantageous to those who
keep on asking Him?*
Matthew 7:9-11

CHAPTER 6

Single. Unfragmented. Whole.

I would recommend that all people were single like me. But, every person has his appropriate gift from God. Some people have the gift of singleness, like I do. While other people have the gift of marriage.
1 Corinthians 7:7

Marriage is a gift from God.
Singleness is a gift from God.

Let's debunk some prevalent myths about singleness and marriage so we can all relax a little more, and let's discuss truth:

- Singleness isn't "waiting in line" to get onto the "ride in the amusement park" of marriage.

- Singleness isn't a punishment, and marriage isn't a promotion.

- Singleness doesn't imply immaturity or inferiority.

- We aren't in singleness, trying to be good enough to be awarded marriage.

"When you get that together," I've heard suggested, "God will give you a husband." I've also heard, "You're struggling with this, so that's why you're not married." I haven't found any Biblical evidence which supports any of this.

First, if we're seeking what we think is spiritual maturity for the purpose of "getting" a husband, we are very wrong. That is manipulation and we are deceived because we will never be able to manipulate God. He's too wise.

Secondly, I believe this "get it together, then the Lord will bless you with a husband" concept is a lie propagated by the evil one to undermine the single person's peace and satisfaction in Christ with discouragement, feelings of inferiority, discontentment and shame.

So, while I believe that growing up in Christ and mastering basic areas of life before we marry increases our likelihood of having a peaceful and successful marriage (just as maturation and such masteries increases our peace and success in every area of our lives), truth is that sanctification is necessary in the lives of the married as well as the single. Each believer is required to cooperate with Holy Spirit to bring about dying to ourselves and living for Him fully at all stages and stations of life. Striving for spiritual maturity is beneficial for everyone who calls upon the name of the Lord Jesus Christ, independent of whether one is married or not. Lack of spiritual maturity negatively affects every area of our lives. But, growing in the grace and knowledge of the Lord Jesus Christ makes all things new and makes our lives more desirable with or without a spouse.

The next topic I'd like to address is our looking for a man.

Ladies. We must come off the prowl.

Acknowledge the objective. The fundamental goal isn't to be in a romantic relationship. The goal is to be satisfied in our soul. With that in mind, it's time for us to stop lurking, ladies. You know we do it. We survey the area for "potentials". We position ourselves to be seated where he's most likely to notice us. We flirt with our eyes, our smiles, our facial expressions, our words, and our body language. We tell other women things like, "Well, he's not going to find me while I'm sitting in my living room." We create profiles on all of the dating sites. We purchase apparel to catch his eye. We join carefully selected social groups, including singles' ministries, Bible studies at churches other than our own and special interest assemblies with this one purpose in mind. We find baby sitters so that we can travel across the country to meet with a man. More often than not, he has an undesirable motive. Yet, many times, we have unethical motives as well. Realize that looking for a man to satisfy us emotionally is no different than a man looking for a woman to have sex with him. Both practices objectify another human being for egotistical, self-serving motives. Every human being has intrinsic value and is loved by God. Using another person to make us happy is evil and selfish. In fact, much of what we call love isn't. Rather, it's an exchange of goods and services to best ensure the longevity of our own satisfaction. We say, "I love you," but often, what we really mean is:

"I appreciate the way you make me feel. Therefore, I'm willing to make you feel good too, so that you'll remain here making me feel good. So, for now, we can barter. But, the minute I no longer have hope that you'll continue to make me feel good, I'm leaving you, hoping I'll find someone else who can make me feel good."

We carry this mindset into marriage. I believe this is why many marriages lack longevity and the people within the marriages fail to make good on their promises of "until death do us part."

I didn't realize, when I vowed to my ex-husband "to have and to hold, from this day forward, for better, for worse, for richer or for poorer, in sickness and in health, until death do us part," that I was nowhere near mature enough to fulfill that vow. My comprehension of what I was saying was as the east is from the west. You know how toddlers can repeat something without any understanding of what it means? Usually, we think that's cute. Well, what I did wasn't cute. I hadn't been married long before I began to transgress my covenant. I was a horrible wife to my ex-husband. Yet, it took Holy Spirit to reveal my flaws to me. For years, I honestly thought we didn't prevail only because of him. I thought he alone was the problem. Moreover, I thought that he was the problem partially because he had failed to make me happy. But I was wrong because it was never, ever his responsibility to make and keep me happy.

Long before he'd ever laid eyes on me, I decided what he should be like, what he was supposed to do for me and how he should make me feel. It didn't matter that I had never expressed those unreasonable expectations to him. They were, I thought, commonplace and he was supposed to be well acquainted with all of my expectations.

See, when I was a very little girl, I was a member of the New Generation Children's Choir of Maryland Avenue Baptist Church in Chicago, Illinois. My childhood bestie and I would sit in the choir stand drawing pictures. We did this to quietly entertain ourselves. Now, I knew from experience that if I failed to quietly entertain myself, my mother was going to give me the look, which clearly meant, "Come meet me in the restroom since you can't act right!" I did not want to meet her in the restroom, so we drew pictures.

I vividly remember the pictures we used to draw. They were usually sketched onto notebook paper. I usually had a blue ink pen.

We always drew pictures
of ourselves
in our wedding dresses.

My friend would draw elaborate, ornate dresses with lace and flowers. My dresses were more of simple elegance. We were gorgeous in our wedding dresses on that notebook paper, week after week.

Even then, I had a mindset to anticipate my wedding. I hadn't even earned promotion to the sixth grade, but at least once a week, my soul was fixated on a fantasy life that included everything that my husband was supposed to be prepared for and happily willing to do. Sorry, James, you didn't stand a chance. Regrettably, my little girl's understanding of marriage didn't mature as I kept having birthdays.

Residing in my soul, but never spoken out of my mouth, my husband's top 12 responsibilities were as follows:

1. Rescue me.
2. Heal me.
3. Create for me a sense of security.
4. Maintain my sense of security.
5. Make me feel beautiful.
6. Make me feel desirable.
7. Make me feel valuable.
8. Keep me encouraged.
9. Always understand me.
10. Keep me satisfied in every way, at all times.
11. Give me his undivided attention when I want it.
12. Instinctively know when I want his undivided attention (which is always because of this endless void I have).

*Disclaimer: This list is hardly exhaustive. It's quite likely that he was tasked with other irrational requirements, depending on my mood. It's likely that some requirements contradicted other requirements. Nevertheless, he was supposed to intuitively know this and perform without error. Always.

Do you see how ridiculous we can be when we try to operate something that's spiritual from a natural, faulty, wounded, confused and deceived understanding? Do you see how absurd our mentality is when we haven't allowed ourselves to be developed in the presence of the Lord? I know I'm not the only one with a list like this. Stats reveal that at least some of the other 40-50 percent of couples had something flawed about their thinking. Come on. We enter marriage with it doomed from the start because our minds, will and emotions aren't spiritually mature. We lack understanding of marriage, its purpose, our purposes, and God's intentions. We're defective. All humans are flawed. Therefore, we contaminate a perfectly good system that God ordained and called marriage, and make it defective as well.

God-ordained marriage is a covenant between a man and a woman who walk together with God. If we look at the example in Genesis, we'll witness the original marriage in the perfect scenario. We see two people who had their own experiences with the Lord prior to coming together. Before God instituted marriage, He instituted His relationship with each individual. We also see evidence that the Lord maintained that relationship with each person separately after they were paired. The Lord was always in the center of marriage because He has to be intimate with each person within the marriage in order for him and her to work properly within the marriage.

Who are we now to think that we can have successful marriages, polluted with self-government, idolatry and independence from God, His mind and His way of doing things? Again, marriage is spiritual, and it requires the inhabitants of the marriage to operate in the fruit of the Spirit for the marriage to produce anything desirable.

The fruit (produce or product of) the Spirit can be described as what the Holy Spirit produces in human behavior when that human has yielded himself to the LORD. The following are what the Holy Spirit produces:

- Love
- Joy
- Peace
- Patience
- Kindness
- Goodness
- Faithfulness
- Gentleness
- Self-control

Initially, during the intoxication phase of a relationship, self-will can fabricate what appears to be the fruit listed above, but this fabrication is sensual, temporal and selfish. Like an addict doing whatever's necessary to obtain the next fix, such is our brain on lust.

Kindness, gentleness, patience—these require a source higher and greater than humanity.

"The report, Police Response to Domestic Violence, 2006-2015, by the Bureau of Justice Statistics, says an average of about 716,000 instances of nonfatal domestic violence were reported to police each year, and about 582,000 instances went unreported. May 3, 2017"
(Source: https://thecrimereport.org)

The absence of sacrifice is selfishness. Selfishness precedes abuse.

Self-centeredness, apathy, and unhealed wounds set up the inhabitants of the marriage to destroy each other and the marriage, but love looks like death and sacrifice. "For God so loved the world that He gave His only begotten son." Jesus came to die. What if we have unreasonable expectations from a spouse and marriage, and don't yet know what love is supposed to look like? What if we still expect marriage to satisfy us? What if this is true for a great number of people in our society? What if these are the reasons the divorce rate in our country is between 40-50 percent, according to multiple sources? (Some report that the divorce rate is declining, but marriage is declining as well. Fewer people are choosing to marry than ever before in our nation.)

- The fruit of the Spirit is required to be successfully married.
- The fruit of the Spirit is required to be successfully single.

Incidentally, I believe the traditional wedding vows are antiquated and produce a bit of a make-believe illusions. I find them indistinct and lacking in honesty and power. I believe the following are more indicative of the vows that I'd like for my husband and I to exchange if I marry. They are specific with an undertone of sincere, deliberate, sober, educated steadfastness. These were found in an article titled, *12 Honest Vows You Won't Hear at a Wedding* on faithit.com:

1. I promise to never flirt, lust, or desire the attention of someone of the opposite sex.

2. I promise to never expect a 50/50 marriage.
3. I promise to make the gospel the mission of our marriage.
4. I promise to love who you are today, not who you want to be.
5. I promise you'll never be responsible for my happiness.
6. I promise to make my expectations clear.
7. I promise to never say, "I forgive you" unless I really mean it.
8. I promise to be for you, to encourage your dreams, to help you become the man God created you to be.
9. I promise to never complain about our marriage, in general, or you, in particular, to others.
10. I promise to believe the best is yet to come, regardless of how good or bad things are today.
11. I promise to protect our marriage from outside influences, including children, work, and in-laws.

12. I promise to surround our marriage with a community of Christians who will encourage and support us.

#13 isn't on their list, but I'd add:
"Until one of us dies."

Because in Malachi 2:16, God says,

"For I hate divorce…"

Then in Matthew 19:8 Jesus says,

"Because of the hardness of your hearts Moses permitted you to divorce, but it was not like this from the beginning."

With these explicit vows, I believe we'll have a better perception of what we've vowed, and we'll know precisely what we're striving to achieve in this very real, messy experience that we call life. Nevertheless, regardless of the vows you favor the most, Holy Spirit and what He produces are still required to accomplish the challenging task of fulfilling their implications. After all, our spouses are imperfect, just as we are. Come, Holy Ghost.

So, let's abandon our quest and trust the divine plan of God for our lives. Let's acknowledge God as the Manufacturer who knows His creation, and what we need to thrive.

Whether we remain unmarried or whether we marry, we do well to trust our loving Savior. I've met women who have been so hurt, abused, rejected, and traumatized that they no longer desire marriage. While sometimes the desire to remain unmarried is a decision based on purpose and righteous desire, some women's refusal of marriage isn't from a healthy place. They are bitter and they are afraid.

You know, I really liked the apartment complex I lived in before I purchased my home. My moving into it was another way the the LORD showed Himself to be for me as I relocated to this city. It was new and I was the first person to have ever lived in the unit I rented. It was gorgeous. The amenities were great. The staff was pampering. It was more upscale than I'd lived in before. So much so that I was only able to afford the smallest unit in the complex. Even though I couldn't really comfortably accommodate overnight guests, I was so happy because my tiny apartment was filled with peace. Nevertheless, there's one thing that always troubled me about that complex, and that was the lack of children. Occasionally I'd see a child, and by occasionally, I mean maybe five times in a year. But less frequently than that, I rarely saw any evidence of them. Seldom did I see a school bus. I never saw any toys or children's bicycles. In fact, we had a dog park on the premises, but no playground. I was a new empty nester, so I understood that neighborhoods and residences cater to different demographics. Yet, no children seemed disturbingly odd to me. I believe this is a sign of our time and culture.

The institution of marriage and family seems to be increasingly less desirable in our time of cyberspace and simulated friendships. People are avoidant of real human connections.

"As part of a recent study, The National Science Foundation (NSF) asked 1,500 people how many friends they had that they could talk with about their personal troubles or triumphs. 1 in 4 said they had **no one** to talk with. That number doubled when they took out family members.

Two-thirds of Americans say they've lost more than 90% of the friends they had 10 years ago. Many Americans can only claim to have 2 close friends — maybe less."

(Source:Why Most People Will Never Have Great Relationships, Mission.org)

The reason, says Mission.org, is "because people can't be bothered to learn how to communicate."

Whether we're communicating with our children, our spouses or our friends, effective communication requires the one communicating to hold communication as valuable. It requires some maturity and enough self-confidence to produce the boldness to be vulnerable, and a good amount of selflessness, gentleness, kindness, meekness and self-control.

Some people would rather barricade themselves away from all of that for a sense of safety. Though, concludes Mission.org, "… isolation and loneliness are far harder (to endure)."

Because of the dichotomy of fear of intimacy and the pain of isolation, some of us mistake a sexual experience for closeness. This is the experience of the fragmented soul.

CHAPTER 7

Let's Talk About Sex

There is no new thing under the sun, according to Ecclesiastes 1:9. The Bible tells of some pretty wicked sexual practices. Take a look:

- 2 Samuel 13 tells us of a young girl, Tamar, who was raped by her half-brother, Amnon. The Bible tells us that Tamar was beautiful and Amnon was in love with her. This "love" is more correctly translated as brazen lust and obsession. He was frustrated because she was a virgin and thought it would be "impossible for him to do anything to her." He consulted his friend who basically told him that he was entitled to anything he wished because he was the king's son. They devised a scheme, whereby, Amnon would pretend to be physically ill and ask their father if

Tamar would be allowed to make cakes to help him feel better. King David sent his young daughter into the house of his son. There, she was raped. After his lust was fulfilled, he "became extremely hateful toward her, for his hatred toward her was greater than the lustful desire which he had for her." He told her to leave immediately. She begged him, terrified of the shame and disgrace, to request to marry her. He called a servant into the room and told him to remove his half-sister from his space. The servant did as he was told and bolted the door behind her. She ripped the colorful garment which rightfully belongs to and indicated a virgin daughter of the king, and went away crying out for help. Her father reportedly failed to properly address the issue. Tamar lost her mind. Another brother, Absalom, killed Amnon to avenge his sister.

- Genesis 19 speaks of an event where the men of the town insisted on raping with the angels who visited Lot. Instead, he offered his two virgin daughters to the mob. When the mob disapproved of Lot's proposal, they lunged at him to rape him. The angels protected him from being taken by the men.

- Later in Genesis 19, the same man, Lot, had no sons. So, those same daughters decided to get him drunk and have sex with him with hopes of impregnation. The elder daughter had sex with her father one night. The next night, the younger daughter had sex with her father. They both became pregnant and gave birth to the children of their father.

- In Judges 19, we're told a similar account of a man who also offered his virgin daughter to a gang of men who insisted on having sex with his male visitor. He told them, "I will bring them (his virgin daughter and the visitor's

111

wife) out to you, and you can abuse them and do whatever you like." When this mob expressed their adamant displeasure, the man shoved the visitor's wife outside of the door. The Bible states the following, "The men of the town abused her all night, taking turns raping her until morning. Finally, at dawn, they let her go. At daybreak, the woman returned to the house where her husband was staying. She collapsed at the door of the house and lay there until it was light. When her husband opened the door to leave, there lay his wife with her hands on the threshold. He said, 'Get up! Let's go!' But there was no answer. So, he put her body on his donkey and took her home. When he got home, he took a knife and cut his wife's body into twelve pieces."

- Mark 6 tells of Herod, who was in high authority, married his brother's wife. John, the Baptist, corrected Herod, telling him that it's unlawful for him to be with his brother's wife. The wife was bitter toward John for this correction, and during a feast, sent her daughter in to dance before Herod. Her dancing pleased Herod and the men who sat with him. Herod was so pleased with the girl's dancing that he offered her up to half his kingdom. Yet, under the leading of her mother, Herod was compelled to give her the head of John, the Baptist on a serving platter.

Those reveal the depravity of their day. Depraved also are the sexual practices taking place these days. Consider these facts, statistics, and quotes:

- According to NBC News "The average male loses his virginity at age 16.9 (years old). Females average slightly older, at 17.4 (years old)."

- According to NSVRC, one in five women and one in 71 men will be raped at some point in their lives.

- As of 2012, according to waitingtilmarriage.org, About 3% of Americans wait until marriage to have sex. "In highly religious groups, up to 20% wait until marriage." That means between 80%-93% of people have sex before marriage.

- Psychologytoday.com states, "...oral sex is commonly regarded as less intimate than intercourse, requiring a lesser level of commitment. For some, it's not sex at all. ...Some even view oral sex as a form of abstinence, as many youngsters practice it as a substitute for sex, and consider themselves virgins."

- fightthenewdrug.org illuminates, "In 2016 alone, Pornhub got 23 BILLION visits. That's 729 people a second, or 64 million a day—nearly equal to the population of the United Kingdom. ... The most popular search term in the whole site was "step mom" for the second year in a row. That's right, incest-themed porn. ...In a study done in 2006 of people age 18-49, 825 looked at pornographic magazines, 84% viewed pornographic films, and 34% viewed pornography online. ...However, times are changing and fast due to—you guessed it—internet porn. In analytics released by popular porn site Pornhub, women are 113% more likely to search the term "hardcore" than men. They are also over 105% more likely to seek out generes of porn like, "gangbang" and "rough sex."

- dosomething.org warns us, "Between 14,500-17,500 people are trafficked into the U.S. each year. Human trafficking is the third largest international crime industry (behind illegal drugs and arms trafficking). It reportedly generates a profit of $32 billion every year. Of that number, $15.5 billion is made in industrialized countries."

cityvision.edu states further, "Slavery takes place within and across borders. The US State Department estimates that 600,000 to 820,000 men, women, and children (are) trafficked across international borders each year. ...What causes trafficking? In a nutshell, there is a demand for it. Men around the world profit in pleasure and in price for the exploitation of women and children."

- en.m.wikipedia.org lists both thirteen countries, including the U.S., as well as international agencies that host organizations that advocate for pedophilia and pederast (adult males who prefer to have sexual relations with little boys).

- From theguardian.com, we learn that the animals that are most likely to be sexually abused by humans are horses, snakes, dogs and cows.

On Thursday 13th Apr 2017, metro.co.uk published an article that reports, "This week, a court heard how 64-year-old Carol Bowditch was filmed as she had sex with dogs and then their owners at anima sex parties in the UK. The case exposed the seedy underworld of bestiality and the people who take part in the extreme activity."

- broadly.vic.com reports, "In May 2015, *Vanity Fair* profiled David Mills, a famous atheist activist and the owner of a RealDoll—a leading manufacturer of sex dolls so realistic they are, to some, indiscernible from the bodies of human women. "I really like women," Mills told *Vanity Fair*, "but I don't like to be around people."

- "She was stoned out of her mind, and they sent her into the VIP room to be raped." States a woman working locally in the adult entertainment industry, with whom I had a personal conversation.

- <u>www.statisticbrain.com</u> lists there are 4,000 strip clubs in the US employing 400,000 strippers.

  According to thelavishgirls.com, "90% of women in the sex industry were sexually abused as children. 70% of interviewees in a study by Sibert and Pine noted that childhood sexual abuse had an influence on their entry into prostitution. 70% of females who are trafficked are trafficked into the commercial sex industry. This includes Porn, Strip Clubs, & Massage Parlors in the US. 89 percent of women in the sex industry said they wanted to escape, but had no other means for survival. Women in the sex industry experience Post Traumatic Stress Disorder at rates equivalent to veterans of combat war."

- Nationalsexstudy.indiana.edu reports that across various age groups and among both genders, between 40-80%

of people masturbated the previous year.

- From the same study listed immediately above, 23 percent of women have received anal sex. Also, four percent of men report that they have received anal sex.

This is not what the Lord intended when He gave us the gift of sex. We have exploited sex so that it looks repulsively different from what God planned it to be. Without exception, and in every possible scenario, the further we depart from the Lord and His will, the more immoral we become in our thoughts and deeds. When driven by baser desires and the pursuit of pleasure (the aspects of ourselves that can never be satisfied), we find ourselves partaking in the acts listed above.

God created sex. He is the mastermind behind the whole concept. He designed it perfectly. The Lord created sex to be beautiful within the structure He intended it. Furthermore, sex is spiritual.

Sex is a phenomenon that we really don't understand and can't fully understand. Just as everything of the spirit, it involves mystery. Godliness, for example, is described by the Apostle Paul as a mystery, even to his son in the Gospel, Timothy:

And without controversy great is the mystery of godliness: God was manifest in the flesh, justified in the Spirit, seen of angels, preached unto the Gentiles, believed on in the world, received up into glory.
1 Timothy 3:16

For those who are faithless, godless, and who walk in spiritual darkness, the understanding of sex is reduced to merely a physical act.

But people who aren't spiritual can't receive these truths from God's Spirit. It all sounds foolish to them and they can't understand it.

*For only those who are spiritual can
understand what the Spirit means.*
1 Corinthians 2:14 (NLT)

In fact, even secular scientists and psychologists have concluded that sex involves, and has a peculiar and tremendous effect on the soul (the mind, will and emotions).

By profession, I'm a Registered Nurse. I've nursed for two decades. I was educated and indoctrinated in the ways of western medicine. The prevalent belief is that everything pertaining to the human body is physical and chemical; at least, that's been my experience. (Coincidentally, because everything is only recognized as physical, there is usually a pharmacological product that is prescribed to correct the issue when disease arises within the human body. For example, if you present three separate complaints to your physician, you're likely to leave with at least three prescriptions.) Yet, as I mature spiritually, I cannot disagree with the statement that everything is spiritual. Everything. I now believe that everything is spiritual and sometimes produces a physical manifestation, but spiritual in origin and in composition.

Sex is no different. There is an attempt to describe an aspect of the sexual experience termed, "sex glue." Herein, is discussed hormones—chemicals such as estrogen, norepinephrine, dopamine, vasopressin, and oxytocin. Chemicals affect the brain. The brain, in turn, affects the mind. These chemicals work together to produce a desire to partake in the sexual experience; that is, intimacy and bonding, pleasure and satiety—feelings of security, trust, and generosity. The Lord of glory, in His wisdom and creative ability, because He loves us and is perfect, has given us the gift of sex. Sex, of itself, is not ungodly; it isn't perverted or bad. Sex isn't dirty or taboo. God is a God of order and structure. He is perfect in all of His ways, and does all things well. Within the confines of God's envisioned structure, sex is brilliant and splendid.

How then has some sex become so contaminated, ugly and destructive?

Saul, who was also called Paul, filled with the Holy Ghost, set his eyes on him (Elymas, the sorcerer), and said, "O, full of all subtilty and all mischief, thou child of the devil, thou enemy of all righteousness, will you not cease to pervert the right way of the Lord."
Acts 13:10

The enchanter, working all kind of trickery, works to pervert the very thing that our Lord and Creator fashioned to bring forth life, bonding and worship of Himself. To enchant means to charm, to captivate or to enthrall. The enchanter bewitches. To bewitch means to cast a spell on and gain control over someone by magic. We allow the enchanter in to bewitch us when we, either knowingly or ignorantly, depart from the ways of the Lord.

Maybe, no one has ever taught us that our bodies don't belong to ourselves.

123

Don't you realize that your bodies are actually parts of Christ? Should a man take his body, which is part of Christ, and join it to a prostitute? Never! And don't you realize that if a man joins himself to a prostitute, he becomes one body with her? For the Scriptures say, "The two are united into one." But, the person who is joined to the Lord is one spirit with Him. Run from sexual sin! No other sin so clearly affects the body as this one does. For sexual immorality is a sin against your own body. Don't you realize that your body is the temple of the Holy Spirit who lives in you and was given to you by God? You do not belong to yourself, for God bought you with a high price. So, you must honor God with your body.
1 Corinthians 6:15-20 (NLT)

Maybe, from childhood, we were so accustomed to being abused that we haven't considered that we have value that is not contingent upon providing sexual pleasure to another person. Or perhaps, along the way, we've decided that providing sexual pleasure is a means to gain or profit. Maybe, the gain we seek is attention, affirmation, acceptance, and the sensation of being cared for and loved. Perhaps, we've never known the appropriate touch of a man, nor his honorable intentions. Therefore, we can't identify what is inappropriate. Still, we're so much in need of a touch that we accept what the charmer, the sorcerer, offers. Thereby, we become bewitched.

The sorcerer has some understanding of the effects of the sexual experience on the female psyche. His understanding is at least sufficient to manipulate. Have you ever considered why, just as you're gaining the fortitude to finally leave a crazy relationship, your lover decides to spend a weekend indoors, away from everything, with all attention on you? These days are filled with sex, bonding, good food and laughter. This is intentional. The Lord purposed sex to bind together the husband and wife.

A newly married man must not be drafted into the army or be given any other official

responsibilities. He must be free to spend one year at home, bringing happiness to the wife he has married.
Deuteronomy 24:5 (NLT)

"Haven't you read the Scriptures?" Jesus replied, "They record that from the beginning. God made them male and female." And he said, "This explains why a man leaves his father and mother and is joined to his wife, and the two are untied into one. Since they are no longer two but one, let on one split apart what God has joined."
Matthew 19:4-6 (NLT)

The intent of the sorcerer is to keep you bound to him for whatever selfish, unholy purpose that fulfills his dark desires. And it works because of the nature of sex and its effects. The Lord creates. Satan perverts. The act is the same producing the same hormonal release, the same effects. It accomplishes the same spiritual outcome. tolovehonorandvacuum.com expounds:

"The part of the brain where oxytocin is released is larger in women than in men. So, during sexual intercourse, the brain releases this chemical that causes the couple to bond on a deep level- but the woman's brain is actually releasing more. Some have suggested that the reason a woman stays with a man who is abusive, or a jerk is because she has a stronger chemical bond toward him. It also explains why, generally speaking, it is easier for guys to hook up and move on without as much emotional turmoil."

Oxytocin is the same chemical that floods the mother's brain immediately after a baby is born, bonding her to her child. Oxytocin is released while a mother nurses her child. It's released when we cuddle, and in social situations where bonding occurs. Take, for example, how close you feel to your friend after you sit at a coffee shop sharing secrets. Oxytocin is released during those times.

But the male brain, on the contrary, produces more dopamine during sexual experiences.

Sciencenewsforstudents.org gives us some insight concerning what dopamine is and what it does:

"The dopamine from the ventral tegmental … usually sends dopamine into the brain when animals (including people) expect or receive a reward. That reward might be a delicious slice of pizza or a favorite song. This dopamine release tells the brain that whatever it just experienced is worth getting more of. And, that helps animals (including people) change their behaviors in ways that will help them attain more of the rewarding item or experience. Dopamine also helps with reinforcement-motivating an animal to do something again and again."

The release of dopamine motivates the male to seek more pleasure, and in many cases, become more indiscriminate in his methods of sexual pleasure. For both genders and their respective brains, we're designed to crave what we gain pleasure from. From a chemical perspective, it doesn't matter if the sexual experience is with our spouse, several people in addition to our spouse, alone, with a Great Dane or with a child—we are designed to desire more of the same. A website (theatlantic.com) tells the story of a man who calls himself "Davecat". He says he has romantic relationships with his synthetic sex dolls:

"It actually didn't take me too long to regard Shichan as a synthetic person, and not simply a thing; it occurred pretty much when I opened her crate for the first time. I was immediately stunned by her lifelike beauty, and after I mentally collected myself, extracted her from her crate, and sat her down on the couch, I just held her in my arms for a while. It felt so right and natural, if you'll pardon the pun. It seemed perfectly normal for me to treat something that resembles an inorganic woman the same way I'd treat an actual organic woman. …Ultimately, getting romantically involved with an organic woman doesn't seem worth it to me."

This may seem bizarre to some of us, but it doesn't miss the mark intended for us by our loving God any more than other methods of seeking sexual pleasure outside of the confines of marriage. Reportedly, this man had parental issues and rejection issues. It appears he has crippling fears, poor coping mechanisms and a chronic lack of appropriate community and socialization. He doesn't know the love of Jesus. Subsequently, he's turned to inanimate objects to pour his affection upon. He desires sexual release with something that he's deemed safe and accepting. He's fantasized that these dolls love him in return, desire him and are eager to please him. This apparently has become his reality.

Regardless of how unusual the practice is, the dopamine release creates a craving. Fulfilling the craving reinforces pleasure, decreases stress and releases endorphins which decrease the perception of pain. The inability to fulfill such cravings produces sensations of displeasure, including depression and agitation. Continuing to fulfill the craving produces addiction. Addiction to one mode of sexual fulfillment often makes one sexually unresponsive to other means of stimulation.

This is why people who are addicted to pornography, for example, cannot become aroused with their physical partner without watching pornography. Or, they may seek to have their physical partner behave in a manner that is consistent with those who act in pornography. This is also why, for example, a person who's accustomed to multiple sexual partners cannot be satisfied with only one. Their brains have been trained to be satisfied only with multiple people. Getting married does not alleviate these issues. Their minds have to be renewed and it's necessary for these people to undergo the D.I.E. process described in chapter four.

What's interesting, however, is when couples who are sexually untainted marry, then consummate their marriage, they will desire each other with that same intensity and exclusivity. They will only be satisfied with each other. Consider these findings recorded in ifstudies.org in an article curiously named *Counterintuitive Trends in the Link Between Premarital Sex and Marital Stability* (I wouldn't have thought these trends would be counterintuitive at all):

"What, if anything, does premarital sex have to do with marital stability? This research brief shows that the relationship between divorce and the number of sexual partners women have prior to marriage is complex. For women marrying since the start of the new millennium:

- Women with 10 or more partners *were the most likely* to divorce, but this only became true in recent years.

- Women with 3-9 partners *were less likely* to divorce than women with 2 partners; and

- Women with 0-1 partners *were the least likely* to divorce.

Earlier research found that having multiple sex partners prior to marriage could lead to less happy marriages, and often increase the odds of divorce."

Nevertheless, don't dismay. Have faith in God. If you're like me, falling into the "most likely to divorce" category, know that Jesus said,

> *"Consider this! I am making everything new and fresh."*
> *Revelation 21:5 (TPT)*

He's the same yesterday, today and forever.

> *If we say that we have no sin, we deceive ourselves, and the truth is not in us. If we confess our sins, He is faithful and just to forgive us our sins, and to cleanse us from all unrighteousness.*
> *Interpreted from 1 John 9*

King David developed an extramarital relationship with Bathsheba. He impregnated her and unsuccessfully tried to make it appear that her husband was the baby's father. He then arranged her husband's death. Afterward, in Psalm 51, he repented:

"Have mercy on me, O God, because of your unfailing love. Because of your great compassion, blot out the stain of my sins. Wash me clean from my guilt. Purify me from my sin. For I recognize my rebellion; it haunts me day and night. Against You, above all, have I sinned. …Purify me from my sins, and I will be clean; wash me, and I will be whiter than snow. Oh, give me back my joy again. You have broken me- now let me rejoice. Don't keep looking at my sins. Remove the stain of my guilt. Create in me a clean heart, O God. Renew a loyal spirit within me."

A clean heart is what we seek after. A heart that loves the Lord entirely and doesn't commit adultery in our relationship with Him.

"…the Lord said to me, 'Have you seen what fickle Israel has done? Like a wife who commits adultery, Israel has worshiped other

gods up on every hill and under every green tree, and there she behaved as a whore.'
Interpreted from Jeremiah 3:6

When we can be faithful to our God, we will stop abusing ourselves. Then, we can be faithful in our marriages.

The Lord really is faithful to forgive and cleanse us when we enter a process of repentance, re-education, deliverance and wholeness. It is a process.

"Falling in love" is no more than a "bewitching season" facilitated by chemical responses. We've romanticized it so. We seek it so! But consider, if falling in love was a reliable precursor to marriage, there wouldn't be such a discrepancy between the success rates of arranged marriages or betrothals and marriages resulting from two people who've fallen in love (called autonomous marriage). I'd rather the Lord "arrange" my marriage. I'd rather incorporate clear, mature, sober and intellectual reasoning when deciding to marry.

Then, I'll experience the heightened emotions and bonding after we're in a covenant that's supported and protected by all of heaven.

According to a 2012 study by Statistic Brain, the global divorce rate for arranged marriages was six percent—a significantly low number. Compared to the 55 percent of marriages in the would that are arranged, this low statistic shows the success rate of arranged marriages.

Our faulty dating system programs us for divorce. We meet a man, talk, share experiences, and then consider ourselves in a committed relationship. Before marriage, most people have had several, if not dozens, of these relationships. This constant entangling of the soul, followed by a break-up, to be entangled with the next person trains us how to divorce. The human soul is not designed to be mated with various people. Each experience results in scarring that's often evident even after healing has occurred. I doubt any of us, on our wedding nights, will say to our new husbands, "I really wish I'd had more boyfriends before today." I'm certain he wouldn't prefer that.

Satan enjoys perverting something for humanity to become drunken with.

- And do not get drunk with wine, for that is corruption, but be filled with the Spirit. Ephesians 5:18

- Let us behave properly as in the day, not in carousing and drunkenness, not in sexual promiscuity and sensuality, not in strife and jealousy. Romans 13:13

- Woe to you who make your neighbors drink. Who mix in your venom even to make them drunk, so as to look upon their nakedness! Habakkuk 2:15

- And these also reel with wine and stagger from strong drink. The priest and the prophet reel with strong drink. They are confused by wine. They stagger from strong drink. They reel while having visions. They totter when rendering judgment. Isaiah 28:7

- I could see that she was drunk. Drunk with the blood of God's holy people who were witnesses for Jesus. I stared at her in complete amazement. Revelation 17:6

For those like myself, who have already had too many relationships and bear the scars of them all, please know that you are not of less value if you come into agreement with the truth that Christ Jesus has redeemed you. Never believe the lie that you are doomed to accept less than what is good and wholesome because of your past. The One who created you has forgiven you, and because of the finished work of the cross of Christ, though your sins were as scarlet, He has washed you white as snow.

CHAPTER 8

Dating? What's Dating?

Once I asked a room full of men who they each thought was a desirable woman. All of them replied with their favorite sexy celebrity, except one. One gentleman quietly pointed at the television and said, "I think she's the most attractive." I looked and to my great surprise, I saw the character Jill Taylor (played by actress Patricia Richardson) wearing jeans and a flannel, carrying a basket of laundry in the 1990's television sitcom *Home Improvement*.

I thank God. I look back over my life, and as in the fairy tale of Hansel and Gretel, I've come to realize that God has dropped morsels of goodness leading me to Himself. He's shown me glimpses revealing Himself and what truth is. These little nuggets, like the one described above, have taught me huge lessons practically. Holy Spirit allowed that guy to teach me several things. For example, there is a kind of man who values the virtuous characteristics of a wife who tends to her home and a mother who cultivates her children more than superficial beauty.

Who can find a virtuous woman? For her price is far above rubies. The heart of her husband does safely trust in her, so that he shall have no need of spoil. She will do him good and not evil all the days of her life. Her children arise up and call her blessed. Her husband also, he praises her. Favor is deceitful, and beauty is nothingness, but a woman who fears the Lord, she shall be praised. Interpreted from Proverbs 31:10-12 28,3

This woman is whole.

We must give time for our healing. We must allow Father to deal with our traumatizing pasts and unhealed wounds. We must be still to acknowledge that we have been affected by experiences—things we've done, things that have been done to us and things we've been involved in. We can be certain that if an issue is not properly resolved by the Word of God and the love of Jesus Christ, we have only suppressed the matter. Everything suppressed will manifest again.

One time, I was walking from the car to the door of where I lived at the time when Holy Spirit asked me, "Where do you think the roots of this tree are?" It made sense to me that the roots would be directly beneath the tree I stood a couple of feet from. He directed my gaze across the street and said, "The roots of this tree are over there.". He was teaching me about our lives. Experiences produce consequences. Understanding those consequences and how to heal from them require revelation from Holy Spirit to sufficiently address and deal with them. Otherwise, we really don't know the root of what's manifesting in our lives or the lives of others.

Not only is it necessary for us to be healed, we want to ensure that the men we commit to going in the same direction with for the rest of our lives have also experienced this wilderness and healing process. We want men who have been transformed by the renewing of their minds. Anyone can say that they are God-fearing.

Once I met a man in the parking lot of a grocery store. This was during a season, which I'm convinced, the Lord made me invisible to any person of the male persuasion. I once heard someone say, "When God has you in that season, even your pastor will walk right past you." I was in *that* kind of season. Men didn't approach me. Furthermore, I had been in that season for quite some time. Years. So, as this very attractive business owner made small talk and I responded cordially, I was having an entirely different conversation inwardly. I was evaluating. I was listening for Holy Spirit. I was evaluating for consistency in what he was saying. I was assessing. I compared his speech to the voice of the Word to discover similarities or lack thereof. I was discerning. While I didn't like the outcome, I thank God that He allowed me to experience it because I was encouraged by my growth. During our approximately twenty-minute conversation, I realized this was a man I couldn't allow in my life. Neither did I want to after evaluating the situation. Initially, he referred to a "Higher Power in the universe." Yet, when I said something about the Lord, his speech became laced with verbiage such as, "Praise the Lord" and "God is good all the time" and "The Spirit was leading me."

This man was a trickster.

With polite but direct probing, people will divulge enough information for us to perceive their character. I was once taught the practice of "Just let them talk. The mouth will advertise the thoughts." Yet, often as women, we're reluctant to ask revealing questions because we're so excited that someone is giving us attention that we don't want to do anything to deter them from participating in the fantasy we've already begun building in our minds.

Nevertheless, by the end of that conversation, he'd told me that he was divorced. Since that time, he had been living with a woman who was caring for him financially. But he was displeased with this woman, he said. He was irritated because she expected him to spend time with her and tell her his whereabouts. This man was using the woman and was ready to replace her. I wasn't interested in inheriting the headache he was giving her.

So, I challenged his thoughts about her and their circumstances. Why, I asked him, wouldn't she expect these things when you're playing the role of her husband? Why, I asked him, have you allowed her to develop the mindset that she has? Why, I asked him, are you exploiting a woman for financial gain? That man told me that he had no choice. He said his money was depleted and he needed this woman to help him. So, he felt justified to use her.

I passed on that, suggesting he be honest with the woman. I told him that I wouldn't be part of her calamity and add to her distress. But, I believe that before my time of entering a season of healing, I would've been enamored with the attention, the fact that he worked with at-risk youth, and he said something about God.

Our perspective literally shifts when we move from a place of dry, barren desperation to a place of wholeness. Jesus came that we could have life, and life more abundantly. Jesus, the Living Water, comes so we won't be thirsty.

If a man hasn't been through his process, he'll be as the man mentioned above. Adam had become well acquainted with the Lord before he was presented with Eve. Adam had been positioned by God in the Garden of Eden and given work. Adam had received instruction. Only after that did God initiate Adam's transition into marriage when God determined it was no longer good for Adam to be alone.

We perform disservices to the brethren when we won't leave them alone long enough for

145

them to understand who they are and what their purpose is in the Earth. Before they understand their work and before they have a foundation of intimacy with the Lord, we are wise to back off. We have all had our ideologies contaminated by the world. God must be allowed to come in and correct the sexual miseducation he gained from his favorite porn stars, what he's learned about marriage from his parents' divorce, and what he thinks a real man is versus what his philandering uncle taught him. Holy Spirit must root out everything that's unlike God, and He must also heal him. He must be healed from being touched inappropriately by his mother's boyfriend. He must be delivered from rejection and the low self-esteem he's suffered through. He must understand why he uses a plethora woman to gain a sense of validation. He must grow to understand that he has sex with so many women because he's learned to finally feel good about himself only when he's in control of another human being.

Other than provide a practical example of a mature woman of God by declining to contribute to his brokenness, the only thing you can do for this man is to pray for him. And I mean pray briefly—from a distance. Speak life over him and move on. Move far away emotionally, with the understanding that you are not Holy Ghost. You cannot heal him. You are not called or anointed to be in his life. To be in the life of this type of man is to be ensnared.

I would be remiss to progress any further without first addressing what I call, *the God Said Lie.*

"God said he's my husband."

This has got to be one of the most diabolical, debilitating, mind-binding tactics from the pit of Hades. Satan loves to use it against women of faith, keeping us distracted and chasing nothing in a desperate attempt to make our deception a reality. I abhor it. I was ensnared

147

by it for years, and it's nothing to underestimate.

It is so very important for the Believer to yield our minds to the Word of God. Women, it is of utmost importance that we harness our imaginations, bringing our minds subject to the truth of God.

We demolish arguments (imaginations) and every pretension that sets itself up against the knowledge of God, and we take captive every thought (and purpose) to make it obedient to Christ.
2 Corinthians 10:5 (NIV)

When we fail to do this, we open ourselves to the trickery of an enemy who has studied every facet of our lineage and us. Our adversary has researched what we desire, what caused us to fall the last time and the time before that, what our inclinations and tendencies are and the pervading disposition of our bloodlines. Our enemy is a skillful and well-prepared strategist, and our only hope of prevailing against the kingdom of darkness is obeying the truth of the Lord our God and His promptings.

Practically speaking, if the God of all grace had not empowered me to decline to move forward with the man from the grocery store parking lot, being ensnared by *the God Said Lie* could've easily looked something like this:

Man: *…so yeah, I'm just working through those things right now, and I just want someone to share ideas with. I can really appreciate a lady like you who can walk with me spiritually and motivate me to continue to develop my program with these boys. She's not spiritual at all. We aren't compatible.*

Me: *I understand what you're saying. We all have things to work through. But, you know you are going to have to face that situation with the woman you're involved with. I know how it is to be with someone you really can't connect with.*

Man: I knew someone with your maturity would see it like that. See, so many women are high-minded. They don't want to be there to help a man build. They just want to come in when the man has it all together. I really enjoy talking with you.

Me: The Lord has been really patient with me. He wants us to be patient with each other.

Man: Hallelujah. Yes, Lord. Can I call you tomorrow? I'd like to spend some time with you.

So, we depart the parking lot, and before I get on the highway, I'm imagining us having a wonderful time on a date and moving forward in life together. Meanwhile, I can't hear truth that Holy Spirit is using to warn me, because my soul is too loud. My mind, will and emotions are becoming activated to support the concept that this man is the one who will rescue me from all my soul's deficiencies. I like the way that feels. I become less acquainted with the reality of the situation because of the pleasure that the fantasy provides. My soul produces dreams about this man because I've meditated on him so. I believe they're dreams from the Lord. I have had prophetic dreams in the past that were according to the Word of God, so I accept the dream as being instructional and foretelling.

For God speaks once, and even twice. Yet, no one notices it. (Until) in a dream, a vision of the night, one may hear God's voice. When deep sleep falls on men while slumbering upon the bed. Then, He opens the ears of men and seals their instruction.
Job 33:14-15

But dreams of me progressing with this man cannot be from God because to do so would be contrary to the Word of God, and therefore His counsel. God is consistent and everything He does and speaks and inspires is consistent with His Word. He is the Word. The Lord our God is one. He is not confused. He does not deviate from Himself. Nor does he alter truth to suit our desires.

*For this is what the Lord of host, the God of Israel is saying, "Let not your false prophets and the psychics who are among you deceive you. **Neither hearken to your dreams which you cause yourself to dream**. For they prophesy falsely unto you in my Name. I have not sent them." Says the Lord.*
Interpreted from Jeremiah 29:8-9

Then the father of lies whispers:

"This is the man whom I have sent unto you to be your husband. Be faithful unto the vision I've given until he submits himself to what I shall also reveal unto him. I am preparing him for you. Only be thou steadfast and immovable."

And, that's it.

The seed has been planted. Because I want to believe it, I accept it with my whole heart. Certainly, the true character of the man will begin to manifest. The relationship will become taxing and obviously unhealthy. My friends and close loved-ones will begin to comment on their concern about my relationship with the guy, and they will begin to question my judgment. But, I would believe that he is in the process of being changed by the Lord and that my instructions from God are to patiently wait for the man to come into agreement with what the Lord will tell him. I would believe that if I endured for a season, the Lord would bring us into a blessed marriage.

Hope is a curious thing. Perverted faith is dangerous. The man appreciates being worshiped, so he continues to toy with me. He abuses me, but rewards me with apologies, compliments, sex, gifts and enough quality time for me to remain hopeful. Satan would continue to speak to me, reinforcing the lie that this man is my husband and that God wants me to be faithful to him. In fact, giving up on this man would be an act of disobedience. Yes! Giving up on this man would even be an act of rebellion. Eventually, I cannot even discern the voice of God because the voice I've become more acquainted with is the voice of the adversary. I listen attentively for Satan's voice because I still, somehow, take pleasure in what he's saying.

I believe I'm fighting a war for my marriage against doubt, unbelief and all the people who say they love me, but refuse to fight with me. I cast down any thought I may think that is not in support of me marrying this man, thinking those thoughts are from the adversary. I distance myself from those who try to warn me and rescue me from this trap, thinking they are from Satan and they, like Satan, don't want the Word of the Lord to come to pass for my life. They don't know him, I think, nor do they understand what God is doing in us. Each time I'm in a church service where faith is being taught, I believe the teaching is from God to encourage me not to give up on this man and our relationship. I reinforce the deception. I fortify it. I become consumed by it until every prayer I pray is in support of it. I won't relent until I am delivered.

A friend once called it "a strong delusion."

The Lord says this:

You were worn out by all your (extreme)
efforts. Yet, you wouldn't say, "This is useless!"
You found new strength. Therefore, you
weren't tired. Whom did you dread and fear so
that you lied? Didn't you remember me or give
me a thought?
Isaiah 51:10-11 (CEB)

Woman of the Most High God, I want to warn
you with the strongest of caution, do not
become entangled with *the God Said Lie*.
Adhere to the basics and you'll become much
more difficult for the enemy to confuse. Violate
the basics and you'll open the door to the
deceiver by rejecting truth. Rejecting truth is
rebellion. Rebellion carries severe and
substantial consequences:

For rebellion is as the sin of witchcraft, and
stubbornness is as the iniquity and idolatry.
Because you have rejected the Word of God,
he has also rejected you from being king.
1 Samuel 15:23

An evil person seeks only rebellion. Therefore, a cruel messenger shall be sent against him.
Proverbs 17:11

Why do you call me "Lord, Lord", but don't do what I tell you?
Luke 6:46

But they rebelled against him and grieved his Holy Spirit. So, He became their enemy and fought against them.
Isaiah 63:10

Rebellion is refusing the truth of God and His precepts in order to construct our own way and manufacture our own desires. To manipulate is witchcraft. Whenever we enact Satan's devices, we give him legal access to our lives. Satan is not kind. His only purpose for coming is to steal, kill and destroy. At all costs, we must remain under the safety of the Lord, remembering that all of His instructions are for our safety and He knows all things. We remain is His safety by obeying His instructions.

When evaluating a man for potential courtship, obeying the fundamentals will eliminate most contenders. And remember, we want to submit ourselves to God. We want the devil to flee from us. We want the unrighteous man, the weapon that is formed against us, to run away.

FUNDAMENTAL #1

If the man is legally married in any capacity, he is ineligible. This means that if he is separated, he is married. If he is sleeping on the couch or in a different room, he is married. If he hasn't had sex with his wife in seventy-two years, he is married. If his wife has a boyfriend, he is married. If they have filed for divorce, he is married. Likewise, if you are legally married, you are ineligible for courtship.

He who commits adultery is senseless. Doing so, he destroys himself.
Proverbs 6:32 (CEB)

FUNDAMENTAL #2

If the man is not a Believer who is submitted to the Holy Spirit with the evidence of Godly fruit in his life, that man is ineligible. Also, please note that it takes time for fruit to emerge. Take a season or two to evaluate all of what is being produced before unguarding your heart.

But, the fruit of the Spirit is this: love, joy, peace, patience, kindness, goodness, faithfulness, gentleness, and self-control. There is no law against these things.
Galatians 5:22-23

Holy Spirit is required to produce the fruit of Holy Spirit. It's *His* fruit. We're foolish to expect godly attributes from each other and ourselves unless the Lord is the most prominent influence in our lives. If we're not submitted to the Holy Spirit, this is what is manifested:

When you follow the desires of your sinful nature, the results are very clear: sexual immorality, impurity, lustful pleasures, idolatry, sorcery, hostility, quarreling, jealousy, outbursts of anger, selfish ambition, dissension (discord and rebellion), division, envy, drunkenness, wild parties, and other sins like

these. Let me tell you again, as I have before, that anyone living that sort of life will not inherit the Kingdom of God.
Galatians 5:19-21 (NLT)

Consider further; if you bind yourself together with an unbeliever or one who is not submitted to the leading of the Holy Spirit, you will always be at odds with your husband—unless you perpetually compromise for him. If your Father is the Father of lights (James 1:17), but your husband is of his father, the devil (John 8:44), what common ground do you have?

Don't be bound together with those who don't believe. What does righteousness share with that which is outside of the Lord's command? What relationship does light have with darkness? What harmony does Christ have with Satan? What does a believer have in common with someone who doesn't believe? What agreement can there be between God's temple and the temple of idols? Because we are the temple of the living God, God has said I will live in them and be their God, and they will

be my people. Because of this, come out from among them and be separated, says the Lord. Don't touch that which is unclean. Then I will welcome you. I will be a father to you, and you will be my sons and daughters, says the Lord Almighty.
Interpreted from 2 Corinthians 6:14-18

As a Believer, the desire of your heart should be to move toward the Father in everything that you do. You believe the Word of God, and it is your compass. You desire to please the Lord, and your priority is Christ-likeness. If your husband is an unbeliever, he isn't concerned about any of those things. In fact, they are foolishness to him. Your faith will dictate everything that concerns you, such as what you do with your recreational time, how you manage your money, how you raise your children, and the friends you keep. As a Believer, the Word of God is the final authority concerning all matters. If your husband is an unbeliever he will, at best, try to maintain a good moral compass. Yet, without Holy Spirit, he will lack the power to do so. When discussing the Holy Spirit with His disciples, Jesus said this:

Listen carefully, I give unto you power (authority that you now possess) to tread over serpents and scorpions (demonic forces), and over all the power of the enemy (Satan), and nothing shall by any means (in any way) harm you.
Interpreted from Luke 10:19

If your husband is an unbeliever, you won't even be able to have intelligent and progressive conversations with him concerning the most important aspect of your life. Your home will perpetually lack peace, as your husband is likely to be irritated with your spirituality. You'll either have a huge disconnect from him or you'll become a carnal, degenerating Christian.

Additionally, the man needs to actively run after God with intensity that is sufficient to lead you. Likewise, the intensity with which you pursue the Lord should motivate him. A clear

161

and distinct sign that the relationship is not of God is if while in it, you regress from the things of God. What is of God will draw you into a greater depth of intimacy with the Lord. God will never give us anything to fashion as an idol.

But watch yourself! Don't forget the Lord your God by not keeping his commands or his laws or regulations that I am commanding you right now. When you eat, get full, build nice houses, and settle down, and when your herds and your flocks are growing large, your silver and gold are multiplying, and everything you have is thriving, don't become arrogant, forgetting the Lord you God. The one who rescued you from Egypt (the world), and from the house of slavery (to sin), the one who led you through this vast and terrifying desert of snakes and scorpions, of cracked ground where you were thirsty, the one who made water flow for you out of a hard rock, the one who fed you with manna in the wilderness, which your ancestors had never experienced, in order to humble you and test you, but in order to do good to you in

the end. Don't think to yourself, my own strength and abilities have produced all this prosperity for me. Remember the Lord you God! He's the one who gives you the strength to be prosperous in order to establish the covenant he made with your ancestors. And, that's how things stand right now. But, if you do, in fact, forget the Lord your God and follow after other gods, serving and bowing down to them, I swear to you right now that you will be completely destroyed. Just like the nations that the Lord is destroying in front of you (the demonic forces that he's given you authority over and allow to be slain for your sake), that's exactly how you will be destroyed- all because you didn't obey the voice of the Lord your God.
Interpreted from Deuteronomy 8

FUNDAMENTAL #3

You should submit your relationship to someone who is Holy Spirit-filled, and in authority, who can provide counsel.

We're aware that there are some communities wherein the property owners raise the prices of the homes and apartments to discourage those who they consider to be an undesirable demographic from relocating to that area. Most often, this has to do with a social-economic class of people. Property owners theorize that those who cannot afford the property are likely to be the ones who will devalue the neighborhood with destructive and disrespectful practices. The tactic of raising the price is usually effective.

Well, I too have a tactic to discourage a certain type of man. When a gentleman expresses desire to pursue an exclusive relationship with me, at forty-six years old, I tell him that he must meet my pastors and mentors and submit his idea to them. How we proceed will be determined by his response, as well as the assessment of my pastors and mentors. This has proven to be very effective. I do this for several reasons.

First, it reveals who is a serious suitor from one who is not. Also, as exemplified in times past where the father of a woman would have to give permission to a potential gentleman caller, this demonstrates to the man that I am under a covering. As a woman under a covering, there is a man who is watching for me. I am not some nameless child who is bastardized, without protection, guidance and direction. And, because someone accounts for me, I am accountable to someone. It says to the man, "Someone has made it their business to look out for me. And while it's possible that you might have gotten over on me, you won't get over on all of us. One of us will discern what spirit you're of."

A man can discern the intentions of another man in a manner that a woman cannot. As women, we may be swayed by his charm or good looks because we are emotional, but a man can detect his deceit.

Thirdly, it reveals that he is a man who knows how to submit to authority. This is a quality that usually requires some cultivating in our culture and time. Perhaps, some men find it difficult to submit to a man in authority because of the lack of a father figure, or the distorted guidance of a father figure within the home. It seems that men who struggle with pride, fear and intimidation also struggle with submission to authority. Nevertheless, I understand order. Submission to proper authority is healthy, beneficial.

Lastly, this practice positions us for supervision. You may rationalize that, as an adult, you don't need supervision and that you can manage yourself. I know that if completely left to my own devices and the will of my flesh, I would self-destruct. We always strive to manage ourselves with the fruit of the Spirit of temperance which is discipline and self-control. But you're fooling yourself if you think you'll never become weak. As a wise woman, I identify my weaknesses and practice divulging them to my mentors. I also invite them to correct me and help me maintain boundaries.

I will continue this system of accountability as I enter the process of courtship. I will invite those selected to ask questions promoting my accountability. I gladly welcome this because I want the favor of God in every aspect of my life as well as in my marriage. I want to safeguard, as much as possible, against allowing the sins of perversion, fornication, idolatry and disillusionment to enter in. I want to evaluate this man for marriage while I am sober, and not while drunken with the bewitchment of an illegal soul tie produced by elicit sex or sex acts.

FUNDAMENTAL #4

A man becomes ineligible if he attempts or would consent to a sexual relationship with you. Doing so conveys several very clear messages. He's revealing that he consents to sex outside of the God-ordained specifications of marriage. Giving you a title, a commitment or even a wedding will not deliver him from this core belief.

By attempting to have sex with you outside of marriage, he is also revealing that he is attempting to discount your value, and that he is unwilling to invest in you properly. The King has given very explicit directives for what must be given in exchange for this level of intimacy with you because you are a daughter of the King. You are priceless and adored by the King. He has commanded that a covenant vow be made in the proper manner, making you this man's wife and his responsibility, before he may lay with you.

A man who attempts to have sex with you outside of marriage reveals that he has not developed the fruit of self-control, which is one of the fruit of the Spirit.

A person without self-control is like a city with broken-down walls.
Proverbs 25:28

Anything can enter into a city with ruined walls. You don't want to be bound together with a man that anything can enter into. Anything. Any foul spirit.
Selah.

FUNDAMENTAL #5

A man becomes ineligible if you are doing most of the pursuing.

Ours is an interesting culture where I don't see as much clarity in the realm of romantic relationships as I'd prefer to. Too often, lines are very blurred. Critical information remains unspoken. Things are general and laissez faire. I'll give an example.

This is the third time John and Mary have enjoyed each other's company within the past two months. They enjoy talking on the phone once or twice a week. Sometimes, they text each other, "Good morning" or "Good night." They also exchange funny posts and memes occasionally. Mary finds herself growing quite fond of John. She believes that John might like her also, but she's unsure. When they're together, he's pleasant, attentive and accommodating. Howbeit, last week, she overheard him reply to one of his friends, saying he was leaving to hang out with "a friend." Furthermore, the other day John and

Mary were hanging out. They ran into someone he knew and he introduced Mary to the woman by saying, "Jill, this is Mary. Mary, this is Jill." Mary felt uncomfortable. She felt like she was in the background while he chatted briefly with Jill. Yet, when they walked away, he seemed normal. So, she wondered if she was overacting. She wants to ask him what's going on with them, how he regards her and what direction he wishes to take their connection in, but she doesn't want to pressure him if what she's thinking is more than he has in mind. She doesn't want to look silly or insecure. She doesn't want him to reject her or stop seeing her either, but she's confused.

A mature man of honorable intentions will not allow a woman to be confused. He will not be vague and non-specific. The type of man described above probably has no long-term plans with Mary. It's unlikely that he's seriously evaluating her for marriage. Maybe, you've heard the adage: If a man wants you, you'll know it. If he doesn't want you, you'll be confused.

There was a time when I ran into a former colleague who I hadn't seen in some time. Several days later, another co-worker contacted me via messenger, saying that this man was really attempting to get my phone number. She asked if she could provide it for him. I told her yes. He contacted me, and we spoke on the phone a couple of times. I asked if he wanted to visit my Sunday school class. He said he would, and asked me to attend his afterward. So, we did that. After the class at his church was over, he introduced me to his pastor, and then walked me to my car. En route he said, "Tiffany, I want you to be my lady." I was a bit stunned, but that was very attractive to me. The manner in which he did it felt very honoring. He was forthcoming and concise with his desires and intentions. That was refreshing in the midst of a "Netflix and chill" generation. I was concerned, however, about some of the other fundamentals. Then, it was terminated after he refused to speak to my pastor. Still, he had exemplified what my dad told me when I was in high school, "If he wants to talk to you, he'll call." Translated to be adult-appropriate, "If the man wants you, he will tell you very clearly and his actions will match his words."

If you determine from the beginning that the man is ineligible, I entreat you to cut it off immediately. Suffering has taught me to be very determined not to allow my soul or my flesh to become accustomed to anything that I'm going to need to give up. It's easier not to start a bad habit than it is to break it. Consider the discomfort involved in terminating a romantic relationship. If we already know it cannot progress, we are wise to disallow its beginning. As my grandmother used to say, "Don't make more work for yourself."

CHAPTER 9

The Excavation: Unearthing the Treasure Within

Come to me.
See, I'm not the one who made you feel small
I'm not the one who made you feel afraid
Or ashamed
Who scoffed at you when you were in pain
Or when you messed up
Looked at you in disdain

Come to me
See
When they took your heart
And they abused your trust
When they made you the object of their lust
When they really meant they'd please
themselves
When they promised you "us"
That was none of me

See
Come to me
I know you've been fractured
I know you've been bruised
I know you've been abandoned
I know you've been misused
But not by me
Whosoever shall gather together against you
shall fall for your sake
I promise you that no weapon formed against
you shall prosper
Watch
I am for you

You think I demand more than you can give
And, you think it irritates me to forgive
You think I'm harsh
And hard
And cold
And mean
But, come to me

Come fall in love with me
So you can keep my commands

I give you my Spirit
And a new heart also
I cause you to keep my judgments
And walk in my statutes
Won't you come to me?

Since thou hast been precious in my sight
Thou hast been honorable
And I have loved thee
See
My thoughts toward you are good
Not evil
But of peace
See
What manner of love is this I bestow upon you
That you should be called Daughter of the
Almighty!

My Daughter
See
You cannot repay me
Won't you just rest in my love
There's no transactional account
No ledger
What I did for you was a total bailout

You were bought with a price
You are mine, beloved

I don't disappear
I don't misunderstand
More than your service
Won't you be my friend?

See
I created you
To be enamored with Me
To give you My presence
To experience My
filling your life
Dispelling the darkness and fright
So you could be in awe
Wide-eyed
Jaw-dropped awe
So I could reveal my splendor to you
So you would have the joy of worshiping Me!

Come to me
See
Can a nursing mother forget her baby
And fail to have compassion on her

Well, she might forget
But I won't forget you
You thought I was aloof
You think I'm distant
You look at yourself, and your own failures
And out of frustration, you think
"Why bother?"
But, look unto me
I never cast you away
Come to me
See
I'm your everlasting Father

The LORD God of all, Creator of Heaven and
Earth, the Sovereign God who reigns forever
has placed Himself into each Believer. He has
impregnated you with skill-sets, talents and
solutions to problems inconceivable to those
without revelation. He has gifted you with
artistic abilities that are to bless the whole
world with beauty and splendor. God has
placed in you that which is abundantly
sufficient to enhance humanity and bring great
joy and pleasure to you. But, He is the
mechanism by which these hidden treasures

inside of you may become apparent to the extent that He intends.

But we have this treasure in earthen vessels, that the excellency of the power may be of God, and not of us.
2 Corinthians 4:7

Only our Creator knows the instructions to produce the intended final outcome of who and what He foreknew us to be. We're like a box of puzzle pieces. No one has seen the picture on the front of the box to gain an idea for proper assembly. Only God knows.

Beloved, we are God's children right now; however, it is not yet apparent what we will become. But we do know that when it is finally made visible, we will be just like him, for we will see him as he truly is. And all who focus their hope on him will always be purifying themselves, just as Jesus is pure.
1 John 3:2-3 TPT

Our role is to "see Him." To see Him means to perceive Him or to realize Him. It is our responsibility to position ourselves to grasp and comprehend the LORD. The amazing thing is that the more we relinquish things that He has declared impure, the more deeply we experience Him. In turn, the more we experience Him, the more He reveals Himself to us, and we become like Him.

This "becoming" occurs in our earthly relationships all the time. Surely, you've noticed that you begin to share mannerisms and word choices with the person or people who you spend the most time with. Couples who have been married for some time boast of being able to finish one another's sentences. This is the same concept spoken of in the scripture above. The more intimate we are with the LORD, the more we begin to resemble Him and even sound like Him.

When he had gone out to the gateway, another servant-girl saw him and said to those who were there, "This man was with Jesus of

*Nazareth." And again he denied it with an oath,
"I do not know the man." A little later the
bystanders came up and said to Peter, "Surely
you too are one of them; for even the way you
talk gives you away.*
Matthew 26:71-74 NASB

It isn't our responsibility to accomplish great
and wonderful things in our lives. Our
responsibility is to seek the LORD. When we
do, we can be assured that He will accomplish
great and wonderful things in our lives.

*So above all, constantly chase after the realm
of God's kingdom and the righteousness that
proceeds from him. Then all these less
important things will be given to you
abundantly.*
Matthew 6:33 TPT

When we spend quality, intimate time with Him,
we receive His mind. We share ourselves with
Him, and He shares Himself with us. We
receive the grace that makes the inconceivable
our reality. What once seemed impossible, we

can suddenly do with ease. Like a person kneading dough—by close contact and handling, instead of the hindrances and impurities, he works godliness, power, and an understanding of our authority into us.

With love and gentleness, God, the Creator, cultivates, nurtures and begins to bring forth the remarkable. But, we must position ourselves for exposure to Him for this to be fulfilled. That fulfilling (or maturity) is the Biblical definition of perfection. He's the Potter. We are the clay. He loves us into wholeness. His love reveals to us who we are.

Things never discovered or heard of before, things beyond our ability to imagine— these are the many things God has in store for all his lovers. But God now unveils these profound realities to us by the Spirit. Yes, he has revealed to us his inmost heart and deepest mysteries through the Holy Spirit, who constantly explores all things.
1 Corinthians 2:9-10 TPT

This is when the glory of God can reign in our lives. This is when, instead of living out darkness and demise, our lives and total beings will literally reflect the brilliance of the glorious God. We give our former lives of heartache and death to know Him, and He makes us vessels of praise in the Earth, worthy of admiration.

You are literally purpose. Upon your birth, purpose was deposited into the Earth. Allow Him to bring forth those precious elements out of you for your benefit and the benefit of all mankind. All sorts of giftings, innumerable talents and immeasurable creativity are resident with you. After all, this is why the enemies of God fought so desperately to keep you bound.

To grant consolation and joy to those who mourn- to give them an ornament (a crown or tiara) of beauty instead of ashes, the oil of joy instead of mourning, the expression of praise instead of a heavy, burdened, and failing spirit–that they may be called hierarchies of

*righteousness- lofty, strong, and magnificent,
distinguished for uprightness, justice, and right
standing with God, the planting of the Lord,
that He may be glorified.*
Isaiah 61:3 AMPC

You are greater than your experiences. Won't
you now exchange what is less for the One
who is far, far greater so that you can begin
magnificent living?

Made in the USA
Columbia, SC
15 November 2020